OUR LIFE IN THE CHURCH

OUR LIFE
IN THE CHURCH

Faith and Life Series
Revised Edition

BOOK EIGHT

Ignatius Press, San Francisco
Catholics United for the Faith, Steubenville, Ohio

Nihil Obstat: Rev. James M. Dunfee, S.T.L.
                 Censor Librorum
Imprimatur: + Most Reverend Bishop R. Daniel Conlon
                 Bishop of Steubenville

Director of First Edition: The late Rev. Msgr. Eugene Kevane, Ph.D.
Assistant Director and General Editor of First Edition: Patricia Puccetti Donahoe, M.A.
First Edition Writer: Martha Schaeffer Long
Director and General Editor of Revision: Caroline Avakoff, M.A.
Revision Writer: Colette Ellis, M.A.
Revision Artist: Christopher J. Pelicano

Catholics United for the Faith, Inc., and Ignatius Press gratefully acknowledge the guidance and assistance of the late Reverend Monsignor Eugene Kevane, Director of the Pontifical Catechetical Institute, Diocese of Arlington, Virginia, in the production of the First Edition of this series. The First Edition intended to implement the authentic approach in Catholic catechesis given to the Church through documents of the Holy See and in particular the Conference of Joseph Cardinal Ratzinger on "Sources and Transmission of Faith." The Revised Edition continues this commitment by drawing upon the *Catechism of the Catholic Church* (Libreria Editrice Vaticana, ©1994).

Scripture quotations are from the Holy Bible, Revised Standard Version, Catholic Edition. Old Testament © 1952; Apocrypha © 1957; Catholic Edition, incorporating the Apocrypha, © 1966; New Testament © 1946; Catholic Edition ©1965, by the Division of Christian Education of the National Council of the Churches of Christ in the United States of America. All rights reserved.

The Ad Hoc Committee to Oversee the Use of the Catechism, United States Conference of Catholic Bishops, has found this catechetical text to be in conformity with the *Catechism of the Catholic Church*.

Contents

THE END OF CHRISTIAN LIFE

APPENDIX

A Note to Parents about the Revision

The changes to the eighth grade student text, *Our Life in the Church*, while minimal, attempt to emphasize the scriptural basis of our Faith in accord with Sacred Tradition. New vocabulary is now indicated by bold type, new words have been introduced to enhance each lesson in the revised text, and each definition can now be found both within the chapter and in the glossary. Common Catholic prayers have been included in an expansive list at the back of the student textbook. In addition, every chapter opens with a Scripture passage, important verses supplement the text where relevant, new questions have been introduced, pre-existing questions have been revised for age-appropriateness, and references to the *Catechism of the Catholic Church* are now specified for each question and answer.

Despite the improvements to the series, it is important to realize that, as parents, you are the primary educators of your children. Your active participation in your child's religious education is highly encouraged. As a family, you are the first witnesses of God's love to your child. If you provide a model of Catholic living at home, if as a family you participate in the sacramental life of the Church, and if you pray and attend Mass together, your children are more likely to take to heart the lessons they learn in religion classes at school. Family discussion of current events with a healthy religious perspective will allow your child to grow up with a better understanding of the world around him, and more importantly, help him to be a Catholic in the midst of it. As stated in the General Directory for Catechesis, "family catechesis precedes . . . accompanies and enriches all forms of catechesis" (GDC, 226; Congregation for the Clergy, 1998). Providing your child with a strong Catholic identity at an early age, while not ensuring a lifetime of devotion, will certainly prepare him for the challenges of becoming a faithful Catholic adult.

The *Our Life in the Church* student text is written on a reading level higher than that of the average eighth grader. This is intentional. It is important for children to hear the Good News in a fuller manner than a more simplified version would allow. Please take the time to review the material with your children, to read the text aloud with them, to study the questions and answers, and to examine and discuss the religious art that accompanies each chapter. By lessening the emphasis on individual student reading, there is more opportunity for your child to concentrate on the Gospel message itself as well as the idea that theology plays an important role in all aspects of his life.

Those who have labored in the revision process of the Faith and Life series sincerely hope that it will provide parents, catechists, and teachers with the assistance they need in the task of evangelizing young minds.

PART ONE
The Church

CHAPTER 1

Christ's Abiding Presence

According to the riches of his glory he may grant you to be strengthened with might through his Spirit in the inner man, and that Christ may dwell in your hearts through faith . . . to him be glory in the church and in Christ Jesus to all generations, for ever and ever. Amen.

Ephesians 3:16–17, 21

"I will not leave you desolate; I will come to you" (Jn 14:18).

These overwhelming words of Our Lord Jesus at the Last Supper ring in our ears as they have rung through the ages. Christ suffered the agony of his Passion and the ignominious death on the Cross because of his love for us. He said, "Greater love has no man than this, that a man lay down his life for his friends" (Jn 15:13). He died to save us from sin and to show us the way to glory through taking up our daily crosses. He wanted to lift us up to himself.

But what would happen after Jesus' death, Resurrection and final Ascension into heaven? His friends feared what would happen. Would he leave only a memory of those days when his friends and disciples so keenly felt the joy of his presence among them? Imagine what it would be like if you had been among them and known him.

The disciples on the road to Emmaus said to each other after Jesus parted from them, "Did not our hearts burn within us while he talked to us?" (Lk 24:32). That question shows

something of the mysterious power his words and his presence must have had. Was this loving holy presence of Jesus to be gone for ever from the earth? No, Jesus Christ himself said, "I am with you always, even to the close of the age" (Mt 28:20).

Abiding Presence

A good father does not forget his children when he goes away. He wants to make sure that they will be taken care of in his absence. Jesus' love for us was so great that it did not stop even with dying for each one of us personally. He wanted to continue to take care of us.

How did Jesus provide for us? How is he with us always?

The words to the apostles "I will not leave you orphans" were immediately preceded by the promise that the Holy Spirit would be sent to them. God the Father would send "the Spirit of Truth," also called the Spirit of Love, or the Fire of Love, who would be the soul of his Church. Christ has left us that Church. Christ is the eternal Shepherd and has appointed a

chief shepherd and other shepherds to represent him in the care of his flock.

Christ Founded His Church

It is recorded in the Gospels that many times Christ spoke of the Church in parables or implicitly. But twice he spoke of her explicitly.

1. First Christ said to Peter in front of the other apostles, "You are Peter, and on this rock I will build my church, and the powers of death shall not prevail against it" (Mt 16:18). What did he mean when he said he will build *his*

Church? He obviously meant what he said. He said so with some emphasis and solemnity.

2. In another passage Jesus says that, if disputes and grievances cannot be settled charitably among those involved, they should be brought to the Church and the Church will make the ultimate decision about the argument. If then the offender "refuses to listen even to the church, let him be to you as a Gentile and a tax collector" (Mt 18:17). In other words in the mind of Christ, the Church was to be the final judge and arbiter of whatever questions might arise among his followers.

In both these passages Jesus clearly speaks of his intention to begin his Church. He in fact continues immediately after both these declarations to say to his apostles, "Whatever you bind on earth shall be bound in heaven . . ." (Mt 16:19; 18:18). This is an almost shocking statement. Christ here was actually giving power over heaven, to a select group of twelve apostles. It was a divine authority that he gave them.

So we see that the Church was willed, founded and built by Christ. He said, "I will build my Church." The Church is therefore of divine origin. She is different from any other society or community. No other human society can claim the presence and guidance of the Holy Spirit. The Church is not man-made nor merely human. This is why we call the Church a supernatural mystery.

The Church Has a Structure

Her members are human, to be sure. And God who understands and provides for our needs, made us to live together in community. "It is not good that man should be alone" (Gen 2:18). He also takes into account the universal characteristics of human societies: for instance, that a society needs leaders, a hierarchy (or assistant leaders), members, rules, and some kind of organization. Without these, societies would become chaotic. It belongs to the nature of things that societies cannot function without structure. We see this in a family or in a sports team.

Or take the example of an orchestra. There is a conductor. Then there is the first violinist, who leads the string section, while the clarinetist leads the woodwinds. It is also necessary to have all sorts of instruments, not just one or one kind. Some—for example, the cymbals—may seem to have an insignificant role. But what would it sound like at the crucial moment without them? They

are truly necessary for the music to sound complete.

Using the example of an orchestra as a comparison to the Church we can say that the structure of the whole orchestra, the conductor, the various leaders, the players, and the instruments are absolutely necessary for the sake of the music. The music cannot come through harmoniously without a structure. On the other hand, they would all be mute without the music. The music is the soul of the whole thing. So it is with the Church. The Holy Spirit—the Spirit of Truth, the Spirit of Love—is, as it were, the music. He is the very soul of the Church. So Christ has promised us this heavenly music, the Holy Spirit sent by the Father, coming through the structure of the institutional Church. In the case of the Church, the fundamental structure itself is willed by Christ.

Christ's Church

Through, with, and in the Church, Christ Our Lord is present. She is *his* Church. She is not someone's idea of what is needed, or the decision of some group that it would be a sensible thing to found a community and elect leaders. She is not a mere human construction, something created by man which can be reorganized at will. It is Christ himself who has founded his Church and divinely appointed his apostles and their successors. He has called each one of us through baptism to play a vital role as a living member of the Church. It is through the Church that we receive the sacraments. It is through the Church that we receive the Holy Eucharist, which is the amazing gift of his presence among us.

In this section of the book we will study this Church of Christ in detail—what she is, what she teaches, her order, her members and what, in brief, has been her history.

Q. 1 *What is the Church?*
The Church is the community of disciples, who, through the Holy Spirit, profess the faith of Jesus Christ, participate in his sacraments, and are united in communion with the pastors he has appointed (CCC 815).

Q. 2 *Who founded the Church?*
The Church was founded by Jesus Christ, who gathered his faithful followers into one community, placed her under the direction of the apostles with Saint Peter as her head, and gave her himself as perfect Sacrifice, the sacraments, and the Holy Spirit, who gives her life (CCC 763–66).

CHAPTER 2

The Birth of the Church

"But the Counselor, the Holy Spirit, whom the Father will send in my name, he will teach you all things, and bring to your remembrance all that I have said to you."

John 14:26

The words above, taken from the last discourse of our Lord on the night before he died, contain his promise to send the Holy Spirit to give life to his Church. In the second chapter of the Acts of the Apostles we find St. Luke's account of this great event.

The descent of the Holy Spirit upon the apostles is called **Pentecost** and is considered the "birthday" of the Church. On this day the Holy Spirit appeared—in the form of tongues of fire—to the small community of Jesus' followers who had gathered in the upper room in Jerusalem—the first members of the Catholic Church. The Holy Spirit gave them the grace to preach the Good News of Jesus Christ so that the Church might increase and spread as Our Lord had commanded.

Pentecost was, however, only the final step in God's plan to establish his Church on earth. For thousands of years God had been preparing for this moment when his Church would finally be manifested to the world. There were, in fact, three stages in the establishment of the Church. It was prefigured in the Old Testament, made present during Christ's life on earth, and made manifest to the world on Pentecost.

The beginnings of the Church can be found in the promises God made to Adam after the Fall. God made further promises to Noah after the flood. In fact, the ark, which saved Noah and his family from the waters of the flood, is a symbol of the Church.

With Abraham and the formation of the chosen people, the origins of the Church become more clear. At this stage, God made a covenant with Abraham and his descendants to be their protector. This was the beginning of the "**ekklesia**"—the people set apart—that they might become holy. (Ekklesia is the Greek word for "assembly." It is the word used in the New Testament for the Church. God calls together the "assembly" of his people, the Church, through his word.)

As we follow the history of the chosen people—the Jews—we see even more clearly the early stages of the Church. When Moses led his people out of Egypt God renewed his covenant (now with the whole people), making them into a true nation. Now they began to worship God through a formal religion, with special ceremonies and a certain code of moral behavior, namely, the Ten Commandments. They

now prefigured what Peter said of the Christian Church. They were a "chosen race, a royal priesthood, a holy nation, God's own people . . ." (1 Pet 2:9).

In the laws of the Old Covenant we can see the Church prefigured. This chosen race, a people set apart, was established with a sacred priesthood to celebrate their Liturgy. This worship of God was a corporate act, that is, the action of the whole people. At the head of the chosen race was God himself, but on earth Moses was his representative. Under Moses there was a hierarchical structure. Aaron and his sons were priests and all other priests would come from their descendants, members of the tribe of Levi. All of this was so that this "church" could fulfill its purpose—to make the people holy.

Later in their history God formed his people into a kingdom, renewing his covenant with David, who foreshadowed the eternal King—Christ. This chosen people was now firmly established, with God as King and David as God's earthly **vicar**, or representative, a foreshadowing of the relationship of Christ and the Pope as the visible head of his Church.

God continued to reveal himself and his will to the people through the prophets. Through these prophets God prepared this chosen race for the coming of the Savior, through whom the Church would be firmly established.

"In many and various ways God spoke of old to our fathers by the prophets; but in these last days he has spoken to us by a Son, whom he appointed the heir of all things, through whom also he created the world" (Heb 1:1–2).

When the Son of God became a man and made his dwelling among us, the Church was actually established on earth. Christ laid the foundations as he preached during his public life. First he chose twelve disciples, called apostles, who were to be the leaders of the Church. They were from different backgrounds: some were uneducated—simple fishermen; another was educated and held a position in the government—a tax collector. Jesus spent a great part of his time teaching and forming this group of specially chosen men, the Twelve Apostles. To the multitude he taught in parables, but to the Twelve he spoke directly, "To you has been given the secret of the kingdom of God, but for those outside everything is in parables" (Mk 4:12). His intention clearly was that they would be carriers of his message: "Follow me and I will make you become fishers of men" (Mk 1:17).

One of the apostles, Peter, was chosen by Our Lord to be the leader of all and to be Jesus' representative on earth. After Peter demonstrated great faith, Our Lord said to him, ". . . . you are Peter, and on this rock I will build my church, and the powers of death shall not prevail against it. I will give you the keys of the kingdom . . ." (Mt 16:18–19). By giving Peter the "keys" Our Lord signified the authority that was given to Peter.

At the Last Supper, the night before he died, Our Lord prayed for unity in his Church. He prayed "not . . . for these only, but also for those who believe in me through their word, that they may all be one. . ." (Jn 17:20–21). He also promised to send them the Holy Spirit so

Church Teaching

"The origin and growth of the Church are symbolized by the blood and water which flowed from the open side of the crucified Jesus" (LG, 3).

17

that they might recall all that Jesus had taught them and be able to teach his message. Through these words Jesus made it clear that his Church was to continue after his death.

When Our Lord ascended into heaven, the basic structure of the Church was complete. By his death he merited for us the graces of salvation. We call this the **deposit of grace**, which is dispensed to us through the sacraments of the Church.

The truths that Our Lord revealed during his three years of public life and during the forty days after the Resurrection were given in a special way to the apostles so that they might teach others. This we call the **deposit of faith**.

The last instruction of Our Lord to the apostles, according to St. Matthew's Gospel, mandated the mission of his Church. On the day of the Ascension Our Lord told his followers, led by St. Peter and the apostles, "Go therefore and make disciples of all nations, baptizing them in the name of the Father and of the Son and of the Holy Spirit, teaching them to observe all that I have commanded you; and lo, I am with you always, to the close of the age" (Mt 28:19–20). The Church, in other words, must manifest herself to the world and bring all men to Christ.

Ten days later, while the leaders of the Church were gathered in prayer, this manifestation began. The Holy Spirit, promised by Our Lord, descended upon them, and they were filled with the Spirit of Love and Truth, who gave them the grace to go forth and preach. On this day Peter, as the leader of the Church, preached his first sermon to the Jewish pilgrims gathered in Jerusalem, urging them to be baptized. "Those who received his word were baptized, and there were added that day about three thousand souls" (Acts 2:41). At this point the Church began her mission to the world.

Since that first Pentecost, the Church has grown and spread into every part of the world. The same Church that was prefigured in the Old Testament, formed by Christ, and manifested to the world on Pentecost still exists today, leading men to God. The Church was finally established as "a chosen race, a royal priesthood, a holy nation. . . . Once you were no people, but now you are God's People" (1 Pet 2:9–10).

Words to Know:

Pentecost ekklesia vicar
deposit of grace deposit of faith

Q. 3 *Why did God choose one people from among all nations?*
God chose one people from among all nations to provide a witness of his promise to them (CCC 60).

Q. 4 *Why did Jesus Christ institute the Church?*
Jesus Christ instituted the Church so that men might have in her a secure guide and the means of holiness and eternal salvation (CCC 775–76).

Q. 5 *What is Pentecost?*
Pentecost is the event of the descent of the Holy Spirit upon Mary and the apostles fifty days after Easter. It is the birthday of the Church (CCC 731, 737).

CHAPTER 3

The Nature of the Church

He is the head of the body, the church; he is the beginning, the first-born from the dead, that in everything he might be pre-eminent.

Colossians 1:18

"By her relationship with Christ, the Church is a kind of sacrament or sign of intimate union with God, and of the unity of all mankind" (LG, 1).

We have seen that the Church is a society that was carefully formed by God and began its mission at Pentecost. This society is composed of those baptized persons who profess the faith taught by Jesus Christ and handed down by his apostles and their successors. The members participate in the sacraments given to us by our Lord, and are united with their bishops under the leadership of the Pope.

In order to understand the nature of the Church more fully, we need to examine three significant points: (1) the Church as the Mystical Body of Christ, (2) the marks of the Church, and (3) the reasons Christ established his Church.

Images in the New Testament

Many images used in the New Testament help us to understand the Church. A number of these arise from Our Lord's own words. Christ frequently spoke of the Kingdom that will be established on earth and finally completed in heaven. Several parables, like that of the mustard seed, use this image, showing us how the Kingdom will grow and flourish on earth, or how the wicked and the just will live together in the world but will finally be separated at the end of time. If we reflect on this image, we can see how it pertains to the Church.

In other places Christ uses the image of the sheepfold. We, the faithful, are the sheep, led by human shepherds on earth but most perfectly by the Good Shepherd, Christ himself. In still other places our Lord uses the images of the vineyard, a building, and his bride to represent the Church. How would these be images of the Church? You may need to use your New Testament to help you.

The Mystical Body of Christ

One of the most beautiful images is that of the Church as the **Mystical Body of Christ**. The roots of this image can also be found in the words of Christ. When Our Lord was speaking of the Last Judgment, he told us that we would be judged in part on the basis of our charity toward others—feeding the hungry, clothing the naked, giving drink to the thirsty, and so on. He concludes by saying, "Truly, I say to you, as you did it to one of the least of these my brethren, you did it to me" (Mt 25:40). In other words, we serve Christ by serving others.

In another place, when Jesus sent the disciples out to preach in his name, he said, "He who hears you hears me, and he who rejects you, rejects me . . ." (Lk 10:16). From both of these passages, we see that Christ in some way identifies his followers—the Church—with himself.

There is another passage (Acts 9:1–5) in which the words of Christ are recorded. Not long after Pentecost a man named Saul of Tarsus was fanatically hounding and pursuing the early Church. "I persecuted the Church of God," he later admitted (1 Cor 15:9). One day on the road to Damascus he was knocked off his horse by a light from heaven and heard mysterious words. A voice said, "Saul, Saul, why do you persecute me? . . . I am Jesus of Nazareth, whom you are persecuting." How was it that Saul (later St. Paul) was persecuting Christ by persecuting his Church? Did it amount to the same thing? What was meant by these words?

For the rest of his life St. Paul would think about these words telling him that Christ and his Church are one. This was such a great mystery that its meaning seemed inexhaustible. He later developed this image of the Church as the Body of Christ in his first letter to the Corinthians (1 Cor 12:12–31), his letter to the Ephesians (Eph 1:22–23, 4:4, 5:23–33), and in many other letters.

Our physical bodies have many different parts, which are arranged so that they can work together. All of these parts—eyes, ears, hands, feet, heart, lungs, and so on—form *one* body, and each part must work for the good of the whole. If one part of the body suffers, the other parts share in this pain, while the healthy parts must come to the assistance of the sick parts. If one part—such as an infected limb—threatens the health of the whole body, it may need to be removed.

As St. Paul tells us, the same is true of the Church. The individual members of the Church must help their fellow members. A sin committed by one member hurts the whole. One saint lifts up the whole. "If one member suffers, all suffer together; if one member is honored, all rejoice together" (1 Cor 12:26). Sometimes it is even necessary to remove one member from the Church in order that the whole may remain healthy.

Furthermore, each of the many organs of the body has its own specific function and is arranged in some kind of order. Each has its own task. The eye cannot and should not want to do what the ear does. The hand cannot and should not want to do what the feet do. The same is true of the Church. In the unity of the Body of Christ there is a diversity of members. There are many individuals in the Church occupying special positions and exercising special functions, but all are united in one whole under Christ. The head of this Body is Christ. St. Paul reminds us, "He is the head of the body, the Church . . ." (Col 1:18). It is Christ who unites this Body and whose life we share.

The Church lives from Christ, in Christ, and for Christ. Christ lives with her and in her. As members of the Church, we are joined together by the Holy Spirit who is present throughout the Church.

The Pope is the *visible* head of the Church, representing Christ. The bishops with the Pope teach, sanctify, and rule in the name of Christ. The priests and deacons assist in this work. Lay people, who make up the bulk of the Church, have their special tasks within the Body of Christ. They may, for instance, be the hands that take care of children in their families or help the poor. They may be the feet that go to visit the sick. They may be the tongues that teach their children the ways of God or spread the Word of God to others in the world. They may be defenders of the faith, like St. Thomas More. Each one has his special vocation, and all work for the one Body of Christ. All are called to holiness.

Again, the individual parts of the body form one living organism, which requires nourishment to grow and mature. The Body of Christ, like the human body, must be nurtured constantly by the graces that are received through the sacraments.

Calling the church a "body," however, is not just a figure of speech. The Church is truly the Mystical Body of Christ. *Mystical* here means spiritual. It is also called mystical to remind us of the supernatural character of this society, which is both human and divine. Unlike purely human organizations, the ultimate purpose of the Church is salvation. The goal is heaven. The Church includes the souls in heaven and those in purgatory. The Church helps us to know, love, and serve God in this life so that we can be united with him for ever in the next.

Marks of the Church

The Church, as we have seen, is a visible institution made up of human beings united with Christ as the invisible head. Since the earliest centuries, Christians have believed that there are four signs, or *marks*, by which the true Church can be recognized. These marks are included in the Nicene Creed: "We believe in one holy catholic and apostolic Church."

Let us now examine what each of these four marks means.

One

The *unity* in the Church is striking and is probably the clearest of the marks. This unity is found in three areas.

First, there is the unity of belief. The Church teaches the same doctrines everywhere and always. Throughout the world the members of the Church profess this one faith. The clearest statements of this faith are in the creeds, particularly the Apostles' Creed and the Nicene Creed. There is also unity of moral teaching, based on the Ten Commandments and the teachings of Jesus Christ. These doctrinal and moral beliefs have through the ages always been and will always remain the same.

Second, the Church is one through her unity of worship and Liturgy. There is one sacrifice, the Mass, by which all members are united in worshipping God. The Church is united also in receiving the Eucharist and other sacraments, by which all share in the life of Christ. While there is absolute unity in the *essentials* of worship, there is rich variety in the rituals and ceremonies that surround them, as we shall see later in our studies.

Third, there is unity of government in the Church. All members submit themselves to one divine authority, Christ. Christ promised us that there would be ". . . one flock, [and] one shepherd" (Jn 10:16). The shepherd is Christ, and he is represented by his Vicar on earth, the Pope. The bishops, successors of the apostles, are shepherds. The Pope is the supreme shepherd, and he, together with them, rules the Body of Christ. Christ knew that any community needed a leader to survive, so he appointed Peter to be his visible representative. It is Peter's successor and those bishops in union with him who now govern the Church. We are united to our bishop, and he in turn is united to the Pope.

Holy

The second mark of the Church is *holiness*. The Church is holy in her origin, first of all, because her Founder, Jesus Christ, is holy and is the source of all holiness. The Church is holy also in her purpose, which is the sanctification and salvation of all her members. She has all the means at her disposal to make her members holy. Her sacraments are also holy because they lead to holiness.

Finally, the Church is holy in those of her members who open themselves to grace, God's life, which is given by the Holy Spirit. Throughout history, the Church has been manifested in the holiness of many men and women who have wholeheartedly accepted Christ and his Church. These *saints*, both canonized and un-canonized, are living proofs that the Church

is holy. Christ said, "By their fruits you shall know them." We can see the fruits of the Church in her saints.

It is important to remember that the holiness of the Church does not mean that all members of the Church are holy. Far from it, unfortunately. Most of us fall far short of holiness and many times even fall into sin. In fact, our Church history reveals that there have been many who have led "unholy" lives. But sin is the result of imperfections in our human nature, not in the nature of the Church herself. Despite our failures we must always strive to imitate the holiness of our Founder.

Catholic

The third mark of the Church is that she is **catholic**, or universal. The Church is called catholic because she possesses the fullness of Christ's truth and revelation, and also because she is for all men at all times and in all places. She is not limited to one race or nation. Her members include both the rich and the poor, the educated and the uneducated, the young and the old. The Church founded by Jesus Christ, unlike the pagan religions at the time, was meant to include every human being.

This mark has become more evident as the Church has grown over the centuries. The Church has spread throughout many nations according to the command of Christ. And through her missionary work, the Church continues to manifest this mark of universality.

Apostolic

The final mark of the Church is that she is **apostolic**. This means that the Church originated with the apostles, upon whom Christ built his Church. We have already seen how Christ chose the Twelve to be the foundation of his Church. Apostolicity also refers to the fact that the Church is still ruled by the legitimate successors to Peter and the apostles, namely, the Pope and the bishops. In other words, the mark of apostolicity is made clear by the fact that authority in the Church can be traced in an unbroken line back to the apostles.

The Church is also apostolic in the sense that she professes the same doctrine taught by the apostles, the deposit of faith given to the Church by Christ. This deposit of faith remains the same in all essentials. Thus the Church is founded on the apostles and the teaching given to them by Our Lord.

Why the Church?

We have seen that Christ founded the Church, his Mystical Body, and identified her by four unique and visible signs. But why did he establish this Church? Understanding this will give us a more complete grasp of the nature of the Church.

To begin with, Our Lord was on earth for only a short time. In order to offer salvation to all men, not just those living in Palestine two thousand years ago, he established his Church to continue his work. By his death Our Lord merited sufficient graces to save all men. He then entrusted to Peter and the apostles the power and the means necessary to carry out the work of salvation. Our Lord himself gave the apostles the task of administering the sacraments.

At the Last Supper, for example, they were given the power to celebrate the Holy Eucharist. After the Resurrection, they received the power to forgive sins. And on the day of the Ascension, they were directed to baptize in the name of the Persons of the Trinity.

So that the Church could carry out this mission of sanctification, Christ also gave the Church the powers to govern and to teach. The power to govern is necessary so that our weakened wills will have the guidance and support needed to follow Christ and his commands. This power was indicated when Christ told first Peter, and later all of the apostles, ". . . whatever you bind on earth shall be bound in heaven, and whatever you loose on earth shall be loosed in heaven" (Mt 16:19). The Church, then, has the power from Christ to be the final judge determining what is necessary for salvation and sanctification.

Finally, the Church has the power from Christ to teach, so that we may know the truths that Christ has revealed to us. The Church safeguards us from false teaching. We have already seen that Christ instructed his apostles to go forth and teach what he had taught them. This work is carried on primarily by the successors of the apostles, the Pope and the bishops, and those who share in their authority.

In the next chapter we will consider in more detail the teaching mission of the Church and especially the sources of her teaching. In later chapters we will consider the governing and sanctifying missions of the Church.

Words to Know:
Mystical Body of Christ   catholic   apostolic

Q. 6 *What are the means of holiness and of eternal salvation that are found in the Church?*

The means of holiness and of eternal salvation which are found in the Church are the sacraments, prayer, spiritual counsel, and good example (CCC 1692).

Q. 7 *Which is the Church of Jesus Christ?*

The Church of Jesus Christ is the Catholic Church, which alone is one, holy, catholic, and apostolic as Jesus willed her to be (CCC 811).

Q. 8 *How is the Church one?*

The Church is one in her origin from God; in her founder Jesus Christ; and in her life of the Holy Spirit; and also one in her faith, in the sacraments, and in her pastors (CCC 813, 815).

Q. 9 *How is the Church holy?*

The Church is holy through her founder Jesus Christ and his Holy Spirit, as well as through her holy faith (CCC 823).

Q. 10 *How is the Church catholic?*

The Church is catholic, or universal, in that she was instituted for all men, is suitable for all men, and has extended over the whole world (CCC 836).

Q. 11 *How is the Church apostolic?*

The Church is apostolic in that she was founded on the apostles and continues in their teaching, sacraments, and authority, through their successors, the bishops (CCC 857).

CHAPTER 4

The Teaching Church

They asked him, "Teacher, we know that you speak and teach rightly, and show no partiality, but truly teach the way of God."

Luke 20:21

"This gospel was to be the source of all saving truths and moral discipline. This was faithfully done: it was done by the apostles who handed on, by the spoken word of their preaching, by the example they gave, by the institutions they established, what they themselves had received" (DV, 7).

As we have already seen, Our Lord left to the Church the *deposit of faith*. His final command to the apostles was to teach all that he had instructed them. He relied on his apostles and their successors to carry his message to the world. This is made known to us today through the living voice of the Church—the Pope, the bishops, the priests—even the laity. Each of these conveys to us the message of Christ, especially the clergy, who are, by their office, the representatives of Christ. The Church bases her teaching on the deposit of faith revealed to us by God. Before we look at the source of this teaching we should first consider what is meant by *revelation*.

What Is Revelation?

Revelation literally means to "draw back the veil" or to uncover. God is primarily a mystery to us. On our own we can have only a lim-

ited knowledge of him. However, God has unveiled some of the mysteries about himself so that we might come to know and love him. He has helped us to know who he is and what he expects of us.

In other words, revelation is the communication by God to man of the truths about himself that he wants man to know but that man could never uncover on his own. These truths are known as doctrines or teachings of our faith.

God did not reveal these truths about himself all at once but only gradually with the passing of time. The process of public revelation began with Abraham and ended with the death of the last apostle, St. John.

The first phase of God's revelation can be found in the Old Testament. Because this revelation took place long before the birth of Christ, we call it "pre-Christian" revelation. If we look at the Old Testament, we can see that God gradually revealed more about himself as the centuries passed.

This revelation was completed when God fully showed himself to us by becoming man and living among us. This phase is known as "Christian" revelation. It contains the truths revealed by Jesus Christ to his apostles. These

26

revelations include the most important mysteries of our faith. Among them are the Trinity, the Incarnation, and the Eucharist.

Source of Revelation

"God graciously arranged that the things he had once revealed for the salvation of all peoples should remain in their entirety, throughout the ages, and be transmitted to all generations" (DV, 7). This sacred deposit of the Word of God has been entrusted to the Church.

There is only one single sacred deposit of the Word of God, but from it flow both Sacred **Tradition** and **Sacred Scripture**, the Bible. It is important to recognize that Tradition and Scripture are bound closely together and communicate one with the other. "Sacred Scripture is the speech of God as it is put down in writing under the breath of the Holy Spirit. Tradition transmits in its entirety the Word of God which has been entrusted to the apostles by Christ the Lord and the Holy Spirit" (DV, 9). By means of Tradition, the books of the Bible are known to the Church, and the Scriptures are more thoroughly understood and interpreted.

Sacred Scripture, the Bible, is the written Word of God. It is made up of a collection of books written at various times by different men who wrote under God's inspiration. As we know, the Bible is made up of the Old Testament, which contains pre-Christian revelation, and the New Testament, which contains Christian revelation.

The New Testament, however, does not contain all that Jesus did and said. In fact, the various books of the New Testament were not even begun until some twenty or thirty years after the death of Christ. The apostles began to preach the message of Christ first, and only later were some of these teachings committed to writing. Scripture itself testifies to the fact that the Gospels do not include all of Jesus'

words. At the end of his Gospel, St. John says, ". . . there are also many other things which Jesus did; were every one of them to be written, I suppose that the world itself could not contain the books that would be written" (Jn 21:25).

What Jesus taught his apostles was passed on to their disciples. For example, St. Polycarp of Smyrna, St. Ignatius of Antioch, and St. Clement of Rome all lived during the last part of the first century and the beginning of the second century. Because they were personally taught by the apostles, they are known as **Apostolic Fathers**. Their writings contain some of Jesus' teachings that are not explicitly found in the New Testament.

Over the centuries many varied and contradictory interpretations of the Bible have arisen. Who had the authority to decide which was the right one? It is important to note that the Church—which, as we have seen was given authority by Christ (Mt 16:19) to settle all disputes on earth—is the interpreter of Sacred Scripture. She is the custodian (or guardian) of Scripture and Tradition because she was promised the guidance of the Spirit of Truth.

The Second Vatican Council says, "Sacred Tradition and Sacred Scripture make up a single deposit of the Word of God, which is entrusted to the Church" (DV, 10).

Creeds

An important written expression of Tradition is found in the *creeds*, or statements of belief, of the Church. These creeds are summary statements of the main doctrines proposed for belief by the Church. The earliest of these dates back to very early times and is called the *Apostles' Creed*.

The *Nicene Creed*, formulated at the council of Nicaea in the fourth century, is an expansion and explanation of the Apostles' Creed. In the first creed, and in fact in the early days of the Church, most doctrines were stated in plain and simple language. Over the years questions and difficulties arose concerning many of these doctrines. The later creeds, particularly the Nicene, were written to explain more fully some of these doctrines.

Councils

A second written expression of Tradition is found in the statements of the Ecumenical Councils of the Church. A Church council is a gathering of all the bishops—under the authority of the Pope—to discuss matters of concern to the Church. We call them *ecumenical*, meaning whole or worldwide, because they involve all the bishops. Over the centuries councils have frequently been called in response to controversies over basic doctrines of the faith. The councils have given the Church the occasion to explain more completely and accurately certain beliefs.

The earliest controversies were over the Trinity and the human and divine natures of Christ. The Council of Nicaea addressed these questions. It is evident that when there was a controversy there had to be an arbiter (or umpire) to decide what the true teaching was. Later councils addressed questions about which books were in fact inspired and thus to be included in the Bible, the nature and number of the sacraments, and the nature of the Church. The decisions of these councils clarify or define the teaching of the Church.

The lists that follow contain some of the most important of the Fathers and Doctors of the Church.

FATHERS OF THE CHURCH

St. Ambrose

St. Augustine

St. Basil the Great

St. Benedict

St. Cyprian

St. Gregory the Great

St. Ignatius of Antioch

St. Jerome

St. John Chrysostom

St. John Damascene

St. Leo the Great

St. Paulinus of Nola

St. Polycarp

DOCTORS OF THE CHURCH

St. Albert the Great

St. Alphonsus Liguori

St. Anselm

St. Bernard of Clairvaux

St. Bonaventure

St. Catherine of Siena

St. Francis de Sales

St. John of the Cross

St. Peter Canisius

St. Robert Bellarmine

St. Teresa of Avila

St. Thérèse of Lisieux

St. Thomas Aquinas

Fathers and Doctors
of the Church

The writings of the *Fathers* and *Doctors* of the Church are also written records of witnesses. The **Fathers of the Church** are saintly Christian writers of the early centuries of the Church who are recognized as special witnesses of the faith. Among the more well-known are the following: St. Athanasius, a bishop during the late third century who defended the doctrine that Christ was both God and man against the Arian heresy; St. Augustine, a bishop of the fourth century who converted after leading a life of great sin and became one of the greatest theologians in the Church; and St. Jerome, a monk and a scholar during the fourth century who translated the Bible into Latin, the common language of the people at that time.

The **Doctors of the Church** are the saintly theologians and teachers of the later centuries whose writings are outstanding in guiding the faithful at all times. One of the foremost among these is the great Dominican St. Thomas Aquinas, who lived in Italy during the thirteenth century. Three women are included among the Doctors: St. Teresa of Avila, St. Catherine of Siena, and St. Thérèse of Lisieux. To help you understand more about the Fathers and Doctors, you might want to choose one from the list at the end of the chapter and read about his life.

The writings and decrees of individual Popes are another expression of the teachings of Christ. Some of these are known as **encyclicals**, letters sent by the Pope to the bishops and the faithful, expressing the teaching of the Church on matters of faith, morals, social responsibility, and other important topics.

There is also the "**sensus fidelium**". Literally, this phrase means "the sense of the faithful." This testimony is from what the faithful have believed over the centuries and what the saints have thought, meditated, and believed, and from the actions, prayers, etc. of the faithful.

The Church teaches us that the "whole body of the faithful who have an anointing that comes from the Holy One cannot err in matters of belief. This characteristic is shown in the supernatural appreciation of the faith (*sensus fidei*) of the whole people, when, 'from the

---

CARDINAL NEWMAN

John Henry Cardinal Newman was born in England in 1801. He was an Anglican scholar who founded the Oxford Movement in England in order to reform the Anglican Church. In many sermons, lectures, and books, Newman expounded the "Anglo-Catholic" position. One of his most important works was a book entitled *On the Development of Christian Doctrine,* in which he discussed how the Church's understanding of her Faith deepens over time. His discussion of this question was the most complete treatment of it up until that time.

Eventually John Henry Newman was led to the true Church of Christ through his studies and his writings. Toward the end of his life he was made a cardinal of the Church by Pope Leo XIII.

bishops to the last of the faithful' they manifest a universal consent in matters of faith and morals" (LG, 12).

Development of Doctrine

One last point remains to be made here about the teaching of the Church. Although the deposit of faith was completed with the death of the last apostle, St. John, our understanding of it has developed over the last twenty centuries. We call this the **development of doctrine**. This is the gradual unfolding of the meaning of many things that Christ revealed to us. It is this development of doctrine that we find in the councils of the Church, the writings of the Fathers and Doctors, and the practical experience of the faith among the faithful of the Church. Since the Holy Spirit, who continues to guide the Church, is the Spirit of Truth, any further development can never be—and never has been—in contradiction to any previous doctrine. One example to illustrate this is the definition of the doctrine of the Immacu-late Conception of Our Lady. This doctrine is hinted at in Scripture ("Hail, full of grace," Lk 1:28), was defended by some of the Doctors of the Church, and was part of the *sensus fidelium* for centuries. Yet it was not officially declared until 1854, by Pope Pius IX. It was not a new revelation, but rather an unfolding of one doctrine over time. Something that is implicit in a doctrine becomes explicit, or it can be the logical consequence of a doctrine.

In this chapter we have discussed the sources of the Church's teaching. In the next chapter we will consider the authority of the Church, first, as it pertains to matters of doctrine and the teaching of the Church and, second, as it pertains to matters of discipline, the governing of the Church.

Words to Know:
revelation   Tradition   Sacred Scripture
Apostolic Fathers   Fathers of the Church
Doctors of the Church   encyclical
sensus fidelium   development of doctrine

Q. 12   *What is the Apostles' Creed?*
The Apostles' Creed is the summary and profession of faith in the chief mysteries and other truths revealed by God through Jesus Christ (CCC 187, 194).

Q. 13   *What is a mystery?*
A mystery is a truth revealed by God which is beyond our reason (CCC 237).

Q. 14 *What are the chief mysteries of faith that we profess in the Creed?*

The chief mysteries of faith that we profess in the Creed are the Holy Trinity and the Incarnation, Passion, death, and Resurrection of Jesus Christ (CCC 189–90).

Q. 15 *What is the deposit of faith?*

The deposit of faith is all that is contained in Sacred Scripture and Sacred Tradition, handed on in the Church from the time of the Apostles, and from which the Magisterium draws all that it presents for belief as being revealed by God (CCC 84–86).

Q. 16 *What is the development of doctrine?*

The development of doctrine is the growth in understanding of God's revelation through the study and prayer of believers and the teaching of the Magisterium (CCC 66, 94).

Q. 17 *What is the sensus fidei?*

The *sensus fidei* is a supernatural appreciation of the faith shown by universal consent in matters of faith and morals, as expressed by the whole body of the faithful under the guidance of the Magisterium (CCC 92–93, 889).

Q. 18 *What is an ecumenical or general council?*

An ecumenical or general council is a gathering of all the bishops of the world with the consent of the Pope, to exercise their collegial authority over the universal Church (CCC 884).

Q. 19 *What is an encyclical?*

An encyclical is a pastoral letter written by the Pope and sent to the whole Church to express Church teaching on some important matter. (CCC 892).

CHAPTER 5

Authority in the Church: Teaching and Governing

Let every person be subject to the governing authorities. For there is no authority except from God, and those that exist have been instituted by God.

Romans 13:1

We have already seen that Christ gave his apostles a supernatural authority. He also said very solemnly: "All authority in heaven and earth has been given to me. Go therefore and make disciples of all nations. . ." (Mt 28:18–19). He thus commissioned the apostles to teach and govern his Church, with Peter at their head.

The Pope and the bishops as their successors form the Church's hierarchy. A **hierarchy** is a ranking of those in authority. This ranking in the Church comes to us from Christ. The basic structure was laid down by him and, as the Church grew, the structure was expanded and developed.

At the head of this hierarchy is the **Pope**, the successor of St. Peter, the bishop of Rome, and the visible head of the universal Church. The Pope has **primacy**, or the "first place," in the Church. He holds the primary authority to teach, govern, and sanctify all members of the Church. The Pope is the visible head of the Church. He represents Christ, the invisible head.

United with the Pope in governing the Church are the successors of the apostles, the bishops. With the Pope the bishops are the most important authorities and teachers in the Church. Each **bishop** is a shepherd, deriving his authority from Christ, and he is responsible for governing the local church, one portion of the whole flock.

This is a pastoral work to which they dedicate themselves. It is important for us to understand that in governing they are performing a great service for our salvation. The shepherds are serving their flock, following the example of humble service which was given when Jesus washed the feet of his disciples. In fact, one of the Pope's titles is *Servus Servorum Dei*, which means "servant of the servants of God."

The Pope and the bishops exercise their authority whenever they teach the faithful in their care. Our Lord commanded his apostles to teach all that he had taught. Consequently, the bishops as their successors are fulfilling Our Lord's command when they exercise their teaching office.

Freedom, Authority, and Truth

Freedom is one of the values we most cherish. It is given to us by God and belongs to human dignity. The Church is the great defender of human freedom. You might think that because there is a teaching authority in the Church, you have less freedom. We have to think whether we mean freedom *from* reality or freedom *within* reality. Many people confuse the two. It would, for instance, be foolish to ignore the reality of the law of gravity and in the name of freedom walk off the roof of a tall building. You want to live in reality, which means you want to know the truth. By knowing the truth, you will be truly free.

It is a gift of God's mercy to have an authority whose teaching, inspired by the Holy Spirit, is truth. Christ said: "The truth will make you free" (Jn 8:32).

Free from Error

Because the teachings of Jesus Christ showed the way to eternal salvation, it is extremely important that they remain in their essentials free from error. And so, Our Lord promised the Church, ". . . I am with you always, to the close of the age" (Mt 28:20). He also promised to send the Holy Spirit, who ". . . will teach you all things, and bring to your remembrance all that I have said to you" (Jn 14:26).

With these and other words Our Lord left his Church with the great gift of **infallibility**. Infallibility means that the constant teaching of the Church about matters of faith or morals, as contained in the deposit of divine revelation, will be free from error. This infallibility was given to the whole Church for our benefit so that we could have certainty of truth. If we reflect briefly on the history of the Church, we will see that, even in times of great confusion, the Church's teaching remained essentially unchanged. Why? There is only one explanation —the Holy Spirit given to the Church by Christ has protected and guided the teaching authority of the Church.

Infallibility belongs to the whole Church, which means that the true Church of Christ can never teach a doctrine that is contrary to what Christ taught. But infallibility also belongs in a special way to the legitimate authorities of the Church—the Pope and the bishops. Whenever

which means he is speaking as Pope, not merely as a bishop or member of the Church; and (4) he must be intending to use his authority to pronounce an unchangeable decision.

The doctrine of papal infallibility has been accepted, at least implicitly, by the Church from the beginning. It follows from Christ's promise to St. Peter making him the head of the Church. To preserve effectively the teachings of Christ, St. Peter and his successors would need this guarantee from Christ. It was not, however, *defined*, or officially declared a dogma of the Church, until 1870 at the First Vatican Council. (This represents an example of the *development of doctrine*, which we discussed in the last chapter.) Pius IX exercised this authority when he defined the doctrine of the Immaculate Conception in 1854, *before* Vatican I. Pius XII used this gift when the doctrine of Our Lady's Assumption was declared in this manner in 1950.

Thus two Popes, almost a century apart, defined on their authority a dogma of faith, one definition coming before and one after the dogma of papal infallibility itself was defined. This illustrates an important point. A formal, infallible definition, either by the Pope himself or by an ecumenical council of the Church, introduces no new teaching, no new doctrine. The Pope is not infallible because a general council said so; on the contrary, a general council could say so only because the Pope *is* infallible and the Church has always believed it. Our Lady's Immaculate Conception and Assumption are not true because a Pope declared them so; a Pope could declare them so only because they *are* true and the Church has always believed them. Such pronouncements are simply formal and final definitions of doctrines always held by the Church.

It is important to note two things about papal infallibility. First, not everything the Pope says is infallible. He must be speaking accord-

the bishops in union with the Pope teach or proclaim a matter of faith or morals as something which must be definitively held, these teachings are infallible. They are protected from error. The bishops with the Pope reaffirm in their own dioceses the constant and certain teachings of the Church on matters of faith and morals.

Infallibility of the Pope

Infallibility also belongs in an even more special way to the successor of St. Peter, the Pope. When the Pope speaks alone is he always infallible? Obviously not. He is infallible in very definite circumstances. For instance, he is infallible when the following conditions—which are called extraordinary—are met: (1) The Pope must be speaking on matters of faith or morals; (2) he must be speaking to the *whole* Church, not a particular group or segment of the Church; (3) he must be speaking **ex cathedra** (literally, from the chair of authority),

ing to the conditions laid down. It follows that his private opinions or statements, even those on faith or morals, are not infallible. It is only when he speaks as the Vicar of Christ that he can speak infallibly. Second, infallibility should not be confused with sinlessness, or **impeccability**, on the part of the Pope. The Pope is a human being and, like all of us, he can sin. We have been blessed recently with Popes whose personal holiness is great; in fact, one of them, Pius X, is a canonized saint. Thus, we sometimes expect sinlessness in the Pope and confuse this notion with infallibility.

Magisterium

The teaching office, or duty, of the Church, known as the **Magisterium**, is exercised in two ways: extraordinary and ordinary. The *Extraordinary Magisterium* refers to the solemn and formal exercise of the teaching office of the Pope and the bishops and it is always authoritative. It is infallible when the Pope alone *ex cathedra*, or an ecumenical council of the bishops of the world with the Pope, defines or proclaims a doctrine of faith or morals. We have already seen that both of these are rare; there have been twenty-one general councils in approximately two thousand years, and not every one of these councils has proclaimed infallible doctrine.

The *Ordinary Magisterium* refers to the normal, regular exercise of the Church's teaching office, and it, too, is always authoritative. For this, various forms of communication have been used throughout history. In our times we see the ordinary magisterium used in encyclical letters of the Pope, statements from a **synod** (a meeting of some bishops with the Pope), and individual instruction from bishops to the faithful in their dioceses.

Although the bishops, taken individually, do not enjoy the privilege of infallibility, they do, however, proclaim infallibly the doctrine of Christ. . . .

When, even though dispersed throughout the world but preserving for all that amongst themselves and with Peter's successor the bond of communion, in their authoritative teaching concerning matters of faith and morals, they are in agreement that a particular teaching is to be held definitively and absolutely (LG, 25).

The Church Governs

In our consideration of the Church's authority so far we have been concerned with matters of *doctrine*. Doctrines of our faith are those elements that are the essential beliefs of our faith. The creeds contain many of these doctrines. But the authority of the Church is not limited to matters of doctrine, on faith and morals. The Church also has authority to govern her members. This authority is exercised in matters of *discipline*. The Church, like any so-

". . . If I ask anyone: 'Would you rather have your joy in truth or in falsehood?' he would say: 'In truth', with just as little hesitation as he would say that he wants to be happy. And certainly the happy life is joy in truth, which means joy in you, who are truth, God, *my light, health of my countenance, my God*."

—St. Augustine, *Confessions*, bk. X, chap. 23

ciety, has the right and the need to formulate rules for her members for their own good, to lead them to holiness of life. These rules do not pertain to our beliefs but to our actions.

If we look at some of our Church disciplines we can see how the Church governs us. For example, the Church tells us that we may not eat meat on Ash Wednesday or the Fridays of Lent. This is a matter of discipline and not part of our creed. But we follow this rule because we believe that the Church should direct us in such matters for our spiritual good. Another example is the Church law that requires us to *fast* (abstain from eating), except for good reason, for one hour before receiving Holy Communion. Other examples of the Church's authority to govern are the obligation to participate in Mass on certain Holy Days and the rules concerning certain liturgical rites. Can you think of others? Each of these laws is a legitimate use of the Church's governing power to ensure that Christ's Church and her members will remain strong.

One further point should be made about the distinction between matters of discipline and matters of doctrine. Matters of doctrine are those things in our faith that have been revealed to us by God and thus cannot be changed by us. They cannot even be changed by those in authority in the Church. But matters of discipline are those practices that have developed over time, laws made by the proper authorities, and thus they can be changed by them. This has happened in the past and may well happen again.

Obedience

We, as faithful Catholics, have an obligation to respond properly to the Church's authority. We have an obligation to believe the doctrines of the faith if we wish to be members of the Church. We will never completely understand the great mysteries of our faith. They are rich in meaning and above us, and we must strive to learn more about them, to love them, to study them, and to exercise the virtue of faith.

In matters of discipline we must be *obedient*. Obedience means that we should comply with the will of another who has the authority to command us. We have already seen that the Church has such authority from Christ. Remember that the Church speaks for Christ; the obedience and respect that we show to Christ's representatives are the same obedience and respect we would show to Christ himself.

There may be times when a particular Church law seems unclear or unwise to us. What do we do then? The following analogy will help you understand. The captain of an army is in a position of authority, and the rest of the company must listen to him and obey him when he gives orders. In fact, they trust him to make decisions wisely. While they must understand the orders, it is not necessary that they understand why he makes a particular

---

Prayer

"Almighty and eternal God, you guide all things by your word, you govern all Christian people. In your love protect the Pope you have chosen for us. Under his leadership deepen our faith and make us better Christians. We ask this through Christ our Lord. *Amen.*"

(General Intercessions for Holy Week)

order at a certain time. The other soldiers try to understand why an order is made, but if they cannot, they assume that the captain knows what he is doing. In order to win the battle they must follow his directions.

The faithful in the Church must act like soldiers in an army. We should strive to understand the spirit that animates the law and then obey it. If we cannot understand it right away, we must presume that those in authority do. This is not blind obedience, for we have first tried to understand and then submitted ourselves to those who do. We should try to understand the Church's laws and to obey them in a spirit of charity. The authority of the Church comes from Christ, who told his apostles that his power was being given to them.

Words to Know:

hierarchy   Pope   primacy   bishop
infallibility   *ex cathedra*   impeccability
Magisterium   synod

Q. 20   *Who is the Pope?*

The Pope is the successor of Saint Peter, the bishop of Rome, the visible head of the entire Church, and the Vicar of Jesus Christ, who is the invisible head of the Church (CCC 882).

Q. 21   *What do the Pope and the bishops united with him constitute?*

The Pope and the bishops united with him constitute the teaching body of the Church, called the Magisterium (CCC 888–89).

Q. 22   *Can the Pope teach error when he defines matters of faith and morals?*

No, the Pope cannot teach error when he defines matters of faith and morals because he has the gift of infallibility (CCC 891).

Q. 23   *Can the Pope and the bishops united with him teach error when they define matters of faith and morals?*

No, the Pope and the bishops united with him cannot teach error when they define matters of faith and morals; they are infallible because "the Spirit of truth" (Jn 15:26) assists the Church continually and protects her from error (CCC 889).

Q. 24   *What is infallibility?*

Infallibility is the gift of the Holy Spirit that protects the Church from teaching errors in matters of faith and morals (CCC 890–91).

Q. 25   *How is the Ordinary Magisterium exercised?*
The Ordinary Magisterium is exercised when, in matters of faith and morals, there is a definitive position taught by the Church through the Pope or the bishops in union with the Pope. (CCC 88, 883, 892).

Q. 26   *How is the Extraordinary Magisterium exercised?*
The Extraordinary Magisterium is exercised in two ways: 1) when the Pope, as Supreme Pontiff of the Church, gives an authoritative universal teaching on matters of faith and morals, and 2) when all the bishops in union with the Pope give an authoritative universal teaching on matters of faith and morals through an ecumenical council (CCC 884, 891).

CHAPTER 6

The Visible Hierarchical Church

And they cast lots for them, and the lot fell on Matthias; and he was enrolled with the eleven apostles.

Acts 1:26

We have seen that Christ founded his Church and willed her basic structure. He built her on Peter. "You are Peter, and on this rock I will build my church" (Mt 16:18). Our Lord himself gave us the outlines of the Church's hierarchy. As is mentioned numerous times in the Gospels, Christ chose twelve apostles, and he gave them the power to carry on his work —teaching, governing, and through the sacraments sanctifying the faithful. He said to the apostles,

> Whatever you bind on earth shall be bound in heaven and whatever you loose on earth shall be loosed in heaven (Mt 16:19).

Successors to the Apostles

Christ gave the apostles the mission of evangelizing all nations. Since *all* nations could evidently not be evangelized by the apostles during their lifetime, Jesus was of course addressing all those who would be their successors down through the centuries.

The apostles also understood him in this way, because immediately after the Ascension, as recorded in the Acts of the Apostles (1:15–26), Peter stood up and told the disciples that he and they must choose someone to replace Judas. They chose Matthias. Thus they began to exercise their power to bind and loose by electing the first successor to an apostle.

Christ in his wisdom chose this structure. He knew that the Church, like any society, would need authority to govern. Without it the Church would be in chaos. In the Old Testament we also see a certain amount of structure among the chosen people. There were different tribes with clearly defined territories, and, sometimes, special functions. For instance, priests came only from the tribe of Levi. There were leaders chosen not by men but by God, such as Abraham, Moses, and David. In the New Testament, which is the fulfillment of the Old, we see the establishment of a hierarchical Church, with divine authority. It is important to realize that the Church is not a federal union or democracy where majority opinion prevails, a corporation where managerial skills are uppermost, or an organization where efficiency is first. The Church may use human wisdom, but she is far above human wisdom. She is supernatural in her essential structure. God says, "As the heavens are higher than the

earth, so are my ways higher than your ways and my thoughts than your thoughts" (Is 55:9).

As we have seen, this hierarchical Church started to function at the very outset, after Christ's Ascension.

Later in the Acts we find the account of the Council of Jerusalem (Acts 15). At this council several of the apostles and other leaders of the early Church met to solve certain questions concerning the gentile members of the Church. Both of these incidents show us that the apostles understood Our Lord's command for them to build up the Church.

The apostles received from Christ the fullness of his powers which they, in turn, passed on to the bishops, their successors. In the early Church each bishop was responsible for the Christians in a particular area. As the Church grew, the apostles passed on their power to other men, increasing the number of bishops. It is this same power that the bishops today have received, making them the successors of the apostles.

Church Structure

Today the Church is spread throughout the world and is divided into various *dioceses*. A diocese is a particular community of the faithful, usually established by geographic area. At the head of each diocese is a bishop, whose role is to teach, govern, and sanctify the faithful in his care. Some bishops have received the title of *archbishop*. An archbishop is the head of an important diocese—usually the oldest in a particular area. His diocese is then called an *archdiocese*. The archbishop has the same power and responsibility as a bishop. All of the bishops are united under the bishop of Rome—the Pope, who is the Vicar of Christ on earth. Just as Peter had authority over the other apostles, the bishop of Rome has the authority to lead the other bishops and to teach the entire Church.

As the Church continued to grow in the early days, other men—deacons and priests—were appointed and given a share in his powers by the bishop. This is still true today. Because the bishop cannot personally care for all the people within his diocese, the territory is further divided into *parishes*. The bishop then delegates his authority and the power to celebrate some of the sacraments to the *priests* in charge of these parishes. Each parish is headed by a *pastor*, who usually has one or more assistants to help him care for the spiritual needs of the parishioners. As a pastor (which comes from the Latin word for shepherd), he is to lead and serve the flock entrusted to his care. The pastor's work is one of service. Christ asked the shepherds to give their very lives for those in their care. Like the bishops, priests share in the priesthood of Christ, principally by celebrating Mass and forgiving sins. They do not, however, have the power of the bishop to ordain others to the priesthood. The priest also shares in the teaching office of the bishop when he preaches at Mass or instructs the faithful of his parish.

There are also *deacons*, whose role is to assist the bishop. They, like priests, are usually assigned by the bishop to work in a parish and help in the care of the faithful. The deacon is ordained by the bishop but does not have the power to say Mass. He can administer the Sacrament of Baptism and witness marriages for the Church. He also shares in the teaching office of the bishop through his preaching. The deacon may also help the priest by visiting the sick, counseling the bereaved, or practicing other works of mercy in the diocese.

Some priests and bishops are made cardinals with the job of electing the Pope and being his closest advisors. Some priests are given the honorary title monsignor. These two groups are not steps within the sacrament of Holy Orders as the others are. **Monsignor** is an honorary title given by the Pope to many priests. The office of **cardinal** is also an honor bestowed by the Pope. At the present time most cardinals are chosen from among the bishops of the Church, although at other times in history some were priests or even laymen. The primary function of the cardinals is to elect the Pope, who has for many centuries been elected from among the *college of cardinals*.

In addition to this, the cardinals assist the Pope in the *curia*. The **curia** consists of the many administrative and judicial offices by which the Pope directs the Church. We might think of it as similar, in some ways, to the President and his various cabinet offices. Each of the curial offices is usually headed by one of the cardinals, although some may be headed by a bishop or priest.

Not all of these offices in the Church are essential. Since the bishops have the fullness of Christ's priesthood, they can provide for all of our spiritual needs. Without the bishops we would not have the sacramental life, which Our Lord gave us for our salvation. This simple structure may have been enough for the early Church. However, now that the Church has grown so large, those who assist the bishops—priests and deacons—make it possible for many more people to receive the graces of Christ.

Just as the authority of the Church comes from Christ, so Christ gave to his Church the power to sanctify. In the next chapter we will look at those sacraments that both sanctify us and incorporate us into the Church.

Words to Know:

diocese monsignor
cardinal curia

41

Q. 27   *Who are the chief pastors of the Church?*

The chief pastors of the Church are the Pope and the bishops in union with him (CCC 862, 880).

Q. 28   *What is the Sacrament of Holy Orders?*

Holy Orders is the sacrament by which a man is configured to Christ and is given the power to continue the apostolic ministry as a bishop, priest, or deacon (CCC 1536).

Q. 29   *Who confers the Sacrament of Holy Orders?*

The bishop confers the Sacrament of Holy Orders (CCC 1576).

Q. 30   *How does the bishop confer the Sacrament of Holy Orders?*

The bishop confers the Sacrament of Holy Orders by imposing hands and praying that the Holy Spirit be sent upon the man receiving Holy Orders (CCC 1573).

CHAPTER 7

The Church Sanctifying: Sacraments of Membership

Now you are the body of Christ and individually members of it.

1 Corinthians 12:27

"And the Word became flesh and dwelt among us, full of grace and truth; we have beheld his glory, glory as of the only Son from the Father. . . . And from his fullness have we all received, grace upon grace" (Jn 1:14, 16).

To help us understand the Church's role in the dispensation of grace let us consider for a moment the parable of the Good Samaritan. You may already be familiar with this parable, but today we will look at it in a slightly different light.

A man was going down from Jerusalem to Jericho, and he fell among robbers, who stripped him and beat him and departed, leaving him half dead. Now by chance a priest was going down that road; and when he saw him he passed by on the other side. So likewise a Levite, when he came to the place and saw him, passed by on the other side. But a Samaritan, as he journeyed, came to where he was; and when he saw him, he had compassion, and went to him and bound up his wounds, pouring on oil and wine; then he set him

on his own beast and brought him to an inn, and took care of him. And the next day he took out two denarii and gave them to the innkeeper, saying, "Take care of him; and whatever more you spend, I will repay you when I come back" (Luke 10:30–35).

We know that Our Lord told this parable in answer to a question about who is our neighbor. This parable teaches us a lesson about real charity. However, it seems that Our Lord also

had a deeper message in mind about grace and the sacraments. As the fourth-century bishop St. Augustine explained in one of his sermons, this parable teaches us about our salvation.

Let us suppose that the man who is traveling from Jerusalem to Jericho is Adam, who also represents the whole human race. He was "robbed"—by the devil—of his riches, that is, the life of grace. Just as the man was left half-dead by the side of the road, the human race is weak, fallen, and without the many gifts God intended for us. Most importantly, after the Fall we were unable to attain salvation. The priest and the Levite signify the priests and the prophets of the Old Covenant, who were unable to restore us to supernatural life. Finally, the Samaritan pouring oil and wine on the man's wounds represents Christ, who "pours out" graces through the sacraments to heal our spiritual wounds.

We can see how man can find his salvation through the Church (represented by the inn) and how the bishops in union with the Pope continue the work of Christ until he comes again.

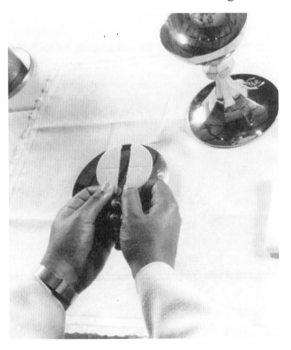

Sacraments of Initiation

The main purpose of all the sacraments is to give us grace and bring us to salvation. However, three of these sacraments are also important to our life as members of the Church. In fact, Baptism, Holy Eucharist, and Confirmation are the sacraments by which we are fully incorporated into the Body of Christ. These sacraments are sometimes called **sacraments of initiation**, since they bring us into the Church and give us full participation in her. They also signify our unity in the Body of Christ.

Baptism

Baptism frees us from original sin and fills us with divine life—sanctifying grace. We receive the Holy Spirit, who then lives in us. It makes us children of God and heirs to the Kingdom of heaven. This sacrament unites us with Christ in a special way, giving us an invisible seal, or mark, which can never be taken away.

Yet the effects of Baptism goes far beyond our own personal lives. Baptism makes us members of the Mystical Body of Christ. In St. Paul's letter to the Corinthians he tells us, "For by one Spirit we were all baptized into one body . . . and all were made to drink of the one Spirit" (1 Cor 12:13). So Baptism makes us members of the Church and unites us closely with all those who have been baptized in Christ.

The next sacrament we will discuss is the Eucharist, which in itself is the most important of the sacraments. First of all, it is a source of spiritual food. This aspect of the Eucharist was prefigured in many ways in the Old Testament —for example, when the manna in the desert nourished the Israelites for many years. In the New Testament, after the multiplication of the loaves and the fishes, Our Lord spoke to his disciples about the "Bread of Life:"

Baptism is also the gateway to all the other sacraments. Once we have become part of the Church we are able to receive from her the graces dispensed through the other sacraments.

Jesus said to them, "I am the Bread of Life; he who comes to me shall not hunger, and he who believes in me shall never thirst. . . . Your fathers ate manna in the wilderness, and they died. This is the Bread which comes down from heaven, that a man may eat of it and not die. I am the living Bread which comes down from heaven; if any one eats of this Bread, he will live for ever; and the Bread which I shall give for the life of the world is my Flesh. . . . Truly, truly, I say to you, unless you eat of the Flesh of the Son of Man and drink his Blood, you have no life in you; he who eats my Flesh and drinks my Blood has eternal life, and I will raise him up on the last day" (Jn 6:35, 49–51, 53–54).

Our Lord tells us here of the necessity to nourish the life of grace born in us through Baptism. Just as our bodies require nourishment, we must "feed" the life of grace through reception of the Eucharist, the *Flesh* and *Blood* of which Our Lord speaks.

Furthermore, the sacrament of the Eucharist is both a cause and a sign of the unity of the Church. The Eucharist causes first our union with Christ and through him our union with one another. All those who receive Christ are truly united through this sacrament. St. Paul affirms this also, in his letter to the Corinthians, when he says, "Because there is one bread, we who are many are one body, for we all partake of the one bread" (1 Cor 10:17). It

is this union with Christ and his Body that is signified by the words *Holy Communion*.

Even the elements of bread and wine chosen by Our Lord for this sacrament signify the very unity that it brings about. Just as many grains of wheat make up the one loaf of bread, and many grapes produce the one cup of wine, so too many Christians are joined into the one Body of Christ through the Eucharist.

Confirmation

The third sacrament of initiation is Confirmation. Confirmation is the sacrament in which we receive the fullness of the Holy Spirit. This enables us to profess and confess our faith as strong and perfect Christians and soldiers of Jesus Christ.

Although we receive the Holy Spirit at Baptism, Confirmation completes what is begun in Baptism and has been nourished through the Eucharist. The new life of grace that we receive, usually as infants, is strengthened in us at Confirmation. At Baptism we were spiritual infants in the Church; at Confirmation we become spiritual adults.

We know from our experience that, as we grow older, we take on more and more responsibilities. When you become an adult, you will have to bear the responsibilities of citizenship —voting, paying taxes, and perhaps fighting to defend your country.

The same is true in the Church. As adult Christians we have the responsibility to bear witness to Christ. This means that we must live for Christ in our daily lives, defend Christ and our faith when it is challenged, and perhaps even die as *martyrs*. The graces of Confirmation prepare us to meet these challenges.

The notion of defending our faith led many of the Church Fathers to speak of Confirmation making us *soldiers of Christ*. St. Paul uses this idea when he writes to the Christians in Ephesus, encouraging them to be strong in their faith:

> Therefore take the whole armor of God, that you may be able to withstand in the evil day, and having done all, to stand. Stand therefore, having girded your loins with truth and having put on the breastplate of righteousness; . . . above all taking the shield of faith, with which you can quench all the flaming darts of the evil one. And take the helmet of salvation, and the sword of the Spirit, which is the word of God (Eph 6:13–14, 16–17).

We must pray then that we use the gift of the Holy Spirit to strengthen and defend our faith always.

As members of the Mystical Body united through these sacraments we have obligations to live as part of Christ's Church. We must accept the teachings of the Church and follow the laws that she has wisely set down.

We must also continuously strengthen our faith through reading and instruction. We know that Confirmation is usually preceded by an intense period of instruction preparing us for our place as adult Christians. However, growth in knowledge and understanding of our faith should not end here. Just as most of us continue our secular education in an informal way after completing school, we must continue our education in our faith. We must strive to deepen our understanding so that we may draw closer to God and our eternal goal.

Rites in the Church

With these three sacraments comes full membership in the Church. But the way the sacraments are celebrated may vary. This is because the Catholic Church is composed of various *rites*. Here a **rite** refers to a common way of worship and of practicing the faith by a particular group of Catholics.

These rites are ancient in origin, and all of them can be traced back, in some way, to the days of the apostles. When the apostles set out

---

Church Teaching

"The Holy Catholic Church, which is the Mystical Body of Christ, is made up of the faithful who are organically united in the Holy Spirit by the same faith, the same sacraments and the same government. They combine into different groups, which are held together by their hierarchy, and so form particular churches or rites. Between those churches there is such a wonderful bond of union that this variety in the Universal Church, so far from diminishing its unity, rather serves to emphasize it. For the Catholic Church wishes the traditions of each particular church or rite to remain whole and entire, and it likewise wishes to adapt its own way of life to the needs of different times and places" (OE, 2).

to "teach all nations," they had received the Holy Spirit and were well-grounded in the doctrines of the faith. But they had not yet settled on the precise forms for the various ceremonies. In fact, these ceremonies developed over a long period of time and reflected the cultures, languages, and history of the various places where the gospel was preached.

As the Church grew, each bishop celebrated Mass and administered the sacraments according to the customs of the city where he lived. Certain cities eventually exercised more influence than others on the surrounding countryside. Of course, Rome, as the center of both the Roman Empire and the Church itself, was the most important. Constantinople (modern-day Istanbul in Turkey) was the center of the eastern half of the empire and became quite important too.

In the Church today there are several different rites. The largest of these—and the one with which you are probably most familiar—is the *Roman rite*, which is used throughout the Western world. It is called "Roman" because the ceremonies originally come from the diocese of Rome. The second-largest rite is the *Byzantine rite*. This rite comes from the ceremonies of the church in the city of Byzantium, or Constantinople—the eastern part of the old Roman Empire. There are also several smaller rites whose origins can be found in other Eastern parts of the world.

These rites are all united under Christ and his Vicar on earth—the Pope. All who belong to them are members of the Catholic Church. The fundamental beliefs are the same, but the expression of those beliefs and the ceremonies vary according to the different cultural origins. To help you understand, let us look at a few differences between the Roman rite and the Byzantine rite.

In the Roman rite, *unleavened* bread is used for the Eucharist, while Byzantine Catholics use *leavened* bread. While Roman-rite Catholics traditionally genuflect before the Blessed Sacrament, Byzantine-rite Catholics have always bowed as a sign of respect. Members of the Roman rite make the Sign of the Cross from left to right; members of the Byzantine rite do so from right to left. The churches of the Byzantine rite are decorated with *icons*. An **icon** is a painting of Our Lord, Our Lady, or the saints, often created on wood and decorated with gold and jewels. The churches of the Roman rite often contain statues in addition to other kinds of images. You will not usually find statues in a Byzantine church.

As you can see, the differences are not in essential beliefs. Both reverence the Eucharist as the Body and Blood of Christ, even though respect is shown to this great sacrament in different ways. This variety enriches the Church, but it also points back to its unity, since all are part of *one* Church.

We have seen that it is through her sacramental life that the Church sanctifies her members. In the next chapter we will consider the form of the Church's worship.

Words to Know:
sacraments of initiation   rite   icon

Q. 31 *What is Baptism?*

The Sacrament of Baptism takes away original sin and fills our soul with sanctifying grace. It makes us Christians, that is, followers of Jesus Christ, sons of God, and members of the Church (CCC 1213).

Q. 32 *What is the matter of Baptism?*

The matter of Baptism is water (CCC 1228, 1239).

Q. 33 *What is the form of Baptism?*

The form of Baptism is the following words: "I baptize you in the Name of the Father and of the Son and of the Holy Spirit." (CCC 1240).

Q. 34 *Who is the minister of Baptism?*

The ordinary minister of Baptism is a bishop, priest, or deacon, but in case of necessity anyone can baptize, provided he has the intention of doing what the Church intends (CCC 1256).

Q. 35 *How is Baptism given?*

Baptism is given by immersing a person in water or pouring water on his head three times while saying, "I baptize you in the Name of the Father and of the Son and of the Holy Spirit" (CCC 1239–40).

Q. 36 *What effects does Baptism produce?*

Baptism makes the baptized person a child of God and a member of the Church by removing original sin and any personal sin, bestowing the life of grace, marking the baptized person as belonging to Christ, and enabling him to receive the other sacraments (CCC 1279–80).

Q. 37   *Does Baptism change us?*

Yes, Baptism transforms us spiritually, causing us to be born into a new life as adopted children of the Father, members of Christ's body, and temples of the Holy Spirit (CCC 1265, 1279).

Q. 38   *If Baptism is necessary for all men, is no one saved without Baptism?*

Without Baptism, no one can be saved. For those who have not been baptized through no fault of their own, the Baptism of blood, which is martyrdom for Jesus Christ, or Baptism of desire (desire for Baptism), brings about the benefits of the Sacrament of Baptism (CCC 1257–60).

Q. 39   *Why can Baptism be received only once?*

Baptism can be received only once because it impresses a permanent spiritual mark upon the soul, which distinguishes a person as Christ's own forever (CCC 1246, 1272).

Q. 40   *What is this permanent spiritual mark?*

The permanent spiritual mark impressed upon the soul at Baptism is a distinctive spiritual mark that will never be taken away (CCC 1272).

Q. 41   *What does this permanent spiritual mark do?*

The mark impressed upon the soul at Baptism sets one aside as belonging to Christ (CCC 1272).

Q. 42   *What are the duties of one who is baptized?*

One who is baptized has the duties of following the teachings of Jesus Christ as found in his Church, including believing the faith of the Church, receiving the sacraments, and obeying the Church's pastors (CCC 1273).

Q. 43 *What is the Eucharist?*

The Eucharist is the sacrament that contains the Body, Blood, Soul, and Divinity of our Lord Jesus Christ, under the appearances of bread and wine (CCC 1333).

Q. 44 *Is the same Jesus Christ present in the Eucharist who was born on earth of the Virgin Mary?*

Yes, the same Jesus Christ is present in the Eucharist who was born on earth of the Virgin Mary (CCC 1373–75).

Q. 45 *What is the matter of the Eucharist?*

The matter of the Eucharist is bread made with wheat and wine made of grapes (CCC 1333).

Q. 46 *What is the form of the Eucharist?*

The form of the Eucharist are these words of Jesus Christ: "This is my Body. . . This is the cup of my Blood" (CCC 1339).

Q. 47 *Who is the minister of the Eucharist?*

The minister of the Eucharist is a priest (CCC 611, 1337).

Q. 48 *When did Jesus Christ institute the Eucharist?*

Jesus Christ instituted the Eucharist at the Last Supper, when he consecrated and changed bread and wine into his Body and Blood and distributed it to the apostles, commanding them to "do this in memory of me" (CCC 1337, 1339).

Q. 49 *Why did Jesus Christ institute the Eucharist?*

Jesus Christ instituted the Eucharist to be the permanent memorial of his Passion, death and Resurrection, spiritual food, and the means by which he is ultimately united with the faithful (CCC 1382).

Q. 50 *How long does Jesus Christ remain within us after Communion?*

After Communion, Jesus Christ remains physically within us as long as the Eucharistic species remains (about 15 minutes) (CCC 1377).

Q. 51 *Is Jesus Christ present in all the consecrated Hosts in the world?*

Yes, Jesus Christ is present in all the consecrated Hosts in the world (CCC 1373, 1377).

Q. 52 *Why is the Most Holy Eucharist kept in churches?*

The Most Holy Eucharist is kept in churches so that the faithful may receive it in Communion, have it for Eucharistic devotion, and recognize it as the perpetual assistance and presence of Jesus Christ in the Church (CCC 1378–79).

Q. 53 *What is the Sacrament of Confirmation?*

The Sacrament of Confirmation makes us more perfect Christians and soldiers of Christ. Confirmation is the sacrament by which God strengthens our faith through the Holy Spirit, sends us out as witnesses of Jesus, and seals our membership in the Catholic Church with the seven gifts of the Holy Spirit (CCC 1285).

Q. 54 *What is the matter of Confirmation?*

The matter of Confirmation is the anointing with sacred chrism (CCC 1293, 1297).

Q. 55 *What is the form of Confirmation?*

The form of Confirmation is the following words: "Be sealed with the gift of the Holy Spirit" (CCC 1300).

Q. 56 *Who is the minister of Confirmation?*

The ordinary minister of Confirmation is a bishop, although a priest may receive special facilities to administer the Sacrament of Confirmation (CCC 1313).

Q. 57 *How does the bishop administer Confirmation?*

The bishop administers Confirmation to the one being confirmed by anointing him with chrism on the forehead, which is done by the laying of hands, and through the words, "Be sealed with the gift of the Holy Spirit" (CCC 1299–1300).

Q. 58 *How does Confirmation make us more perfect Christians?*

Confirmation makes us more perfect Christians and witnesses of Jesus Christ by giving us an abundance of the Holy Spirit, his grace and his gifts, which confirm and strengthen us in faith and in the other virtues (CCC 1303).

Q. 59 *What dispositions should a person who is going to be confirmed have?*

A person who is going to be confirmed should be in the grace of God and ought to know the principal mysteries of our faith. He should approach the Sacrament with devotion, aware that by being confirmed he is being consecrated to God and marked with the Holy Spirit (CCC 1309–10).

Q. 60 *What does the sacred chrism signify?*

Sacred chrism signifies that he who is confirmed is consecrated to God and marked with the Holy Spirit (CCC 1293–95).

Q. 61 *What does the anointing on the forehead in the form of a cross signify?*

The anointing on the forehead in the form of a cross signifies that the confirmed person, as a brave witness of Jesus Christ, should not be ashamed of the Cross nor fear enemies of the faith (CCC 1295–96).

Q. 62   *What are the duties of one who is confirmed?*
One who is confirmed has the duties of witnessing to and defending the faith, and continuing to live his baptismal promises.

Q. 63   *What are the seven gifts of the Holy Spirit?*
The seven gifts of the Holy Spirit are: wisdom, understanding, counsel, knowledge, piety, fortitude, and fear of the Lord (CCC 1831).

Q. 64   *What are the fruits of the Holy Spirit?*
The fruits of the Holy Spirit are: charity, joy, peace, patience, kindness, goodness, continence, mildness, fidelity, self-control, modesty, and chastity (CCC 1832).

CHAPTER 8

The Church Sanctifying: Worship

And I heard every creature in heaven and on earth and under the earth and in the sea, and all therein, saying, "To him who sits upon the throne and to the Lamb be blessing and honor and glory and might for ever and ever!"

Revelation 5:13

"The Liturgy is the summit toward which the activity of the Church is directed; it is also the fount from which all her power flows" (SC, 4).

Men have worshipped their Creator since the beginning of the world. Long before Christianity, many civilizations had elaborate forms of public worship that had been established for centuries. These pagan peoples recognized the need to offer something to their Creator in return for the many benefits that they had received. They also recognized that this worship should be public, since so many of their blessings were received in common. The great civilization of Greece, which rose to prominence in the centuries immediately preceding the coming of Christ, was one that practiced public worship.

The word "liturgy" comes from the Greek and means "public work." Originally, this referred to any public act, especially those done by the wealthy for the benefit of the rest of society. It was understood that people who had benefited were bound to make some return

from these benefits. The wealthy would often sponsor plays or some other work for the whole society. By extension, the word was transferred to acts of worship, since the wealthy would often support these as well. As we will use the word here, **liturgy** means the Church's official public worship. This worship of God must be performed both as individuals and as a people. The Liturgy differs from our private devotions and prayers in being public and in having an external and a formal aspect. It is the action of Christ and his entire Church, rather than the action of an individual. Christ said, "Where two or three are gathered together in my name, there am I in the midst of them" (Mt 18:20).

Through the Liturgy we, the Mystical Body of Christ, are united with Christ in his priestly role to give honor and praise to God. It is proper that the Church as a whole people should do this, since the Church as a whole people was given the graces necessary for salvation. The Liturgy allows us as a whole people to offer to God the highest praise possible, since in it we unite ourselves with Christ in praising the Father. It also adds a new dimension to prayer, since we join in the heavenly chorus of the Communion of Saints, who all belong to the Church. Praying in community lifts up our hearts and increases charity.

Three elements make up the Liturgy: (1) the Eucharist, that is, the Holy Sacrifice of the Mass, (2) the sacraments, and (3) the Divine Office, or Liturgy of the Hours. Each time the Mass is offered, the perfect Sacrifice of Calvary, that is, the whole Paschal mystery, the Passion, death, and Resurrection of Christ, is renewed on our altars. The Mass, then, is the most important element, since it is here that we join most perfectly with Christ offering himself to the Father. We can take part in the Mass most perfectly by worthily receiving the Body and Blood of Christ in the Sacrament of the Eucharist. In the Eucharist, we are nourished with the Body of Christ and, in this way, we become more fully the Body of Christ.

The remaining six sacraments make up the second element of the Liturgy. These are the special channels of God's grace, given to us by Jesus Christ and enabling us to participate in the supernatural life. Over the centuries the prayers and ceremonies that accompany the sacraments have changed, but the essential form was established by Christ himself.

Finally, the public worship of the Church is carried out by the daily recitation of the Divine Office, or Liturgy of the Hours. The Liturgy of the Hours is a prayer of praise composed of Psalms, prayers, instructions, and readings from Scripture and the writings of the saints. These are divided into segments called "hours," each of which is to be prayed at certain times during the day. This enables us to sanctify the entire day by praising God. Priests and other religious have a special obligation to recite, say, or sing the Office, but it is prayed by many lay people as well.

In order that the Liturgy may truly be a sign of the unity of the Church, the Church has laid

down certain fixed and universal rules for its proper celebration. In this way, Catholics all over the world can join together in one act of public worship. These rituals also ensure that the Liturgy is reverent, dignified, and worthy of being offered to God.

The Liturgical Year

Our natural lives are governed to a great extent by the natural rhythm of the seasons. As the year passes, our lives are affected by the seasons in nature. As we pass from one season to another, we must change our clothing, our activities, and even the food we eat. We also notice that the colors in nature change as we move from one season to another, for example, the changing colors of the leaves in autumn. The life of the Church is similar to this pattern in nature. The Church year is divided into seasons as well. As we move from one season to another, our spiritual lives and activities change, just as our natural lives and activities change with the passing of the seasons. As in nature we see the colors change with the seasons, so too, in the Church's year we see a change in colors. This Church year is known as the **liturgical year**. Each division, or season, of the year has its own special prayers for the Mass and the Divine Office. The mysteries of God are so great and inexhaustible that we will always have to continue to grow in understanding and love. Since we are unable to grasp Christ's revelation all at once, our Mother the Church shows us one facet at a time rhythmically during the whole liturgical year. The person of Jesus has so many varied aspects—such as mercy, gentleness, majesty, justice, authority, tenderness, severity, compassion, sorrow, serenity, love, peace, and many more—that we will never come to the end of the mystery that is Jesus, and thus never finish praising him.

The liturgical year is based upon the three major feasts of Christmas, Easter, and Pentecost. (See the diagram on page 58.) These feasts celebrate the principal events in the history of our salvation: the Incarnation, that is, the second Person of the Trinity becoming man; the Redemption, that is, the suffering, death, and Resurrection of Our Lord; and Pentecost, that is, the descent of the Holy Spirit upon the apostles, which is the birthday of the Church. Of these three feasts, Christmas and Easter are especially important, and thus they require periods of preparation as well as periods of celebration. Easter is the most important, and therefore the periods of preparation and celebration are longer. Let us now look at the seasons of the liturgical year.

Advent and Christmas

The liturgical year begins on a Sunday in late November or early December, four weeks before Christmas, with the season of Advent. Advent is the penitential season of preparation that precedes the feast of Christmas. The word *Advent* comes from the Latin word that means "coming."

During Advent the Church meditates on both past and future events. In the centuries before Christ, God's chosen people awaited and kept themselves prepared for the birth of a Savior. Likewise, we prepare ourselves to celebrate Christmas, the feast of his first "coming" among us. During this period, we also contemplate the *Second* Coming of Christ at the end of the world. The Liturgy of Advent prepares us for this event as well.

Advent is a season of penance, since this is the best way to prepare our hearts for Christ. The readings and prayers in the Mass and the Divine Office focus upon this idea and help us to meditate on the two comings of Christ. We hear in the Gospel, for example, the message of John the Baptist about repenting in order to prepare for the Messiah's coming. We also hear the words of Isaiah on a similar theme.

Despite this penitential theme, Advent retains a sense of joyful expectation, since the coming of the Savior is an event of great joy. We should rejoice, since the Savior was in fact born among us. On the third of the four Sundays of Advent, the Church particularly reminds us of this through the liturgical readings and prayers. This Sunday is called "Gaudete Sunday," taken from the Latin word meaning "rejoice."

The season of Advent ends with the midnight Mass on December 24, as the Church begins her celebration of the great feast of Christmas. This feast celebrates the nativity of our Savior and is the beginning of the Christmas season. In contrast to Advent, this is a season of great joy. It includes the feast of the Epiphany, when we celebrate the revelation of Christ to the Gentiles, represented by the three wise men, and it ends with the feast of the Baptism of Christ.

Lent and Easter

The next season of the year is the season of preparation for the feast of Easter. It is called Lent and begins on Ash Wednesday. The ashes we receive on that day remind us of our own mortality. The Lenten season lasts for forty days, a little more than six weeks. The forty days represent the forty days Jesus spent in the desert preparing for his public life. In the Liturgy of Lent the Church urges us, through the readings and prayers, to do penance in reparation for our sins. We can do this through fasting, self-denial, almsgiving, and other good works.

Since this season is so closely linked to the suffering and death of Our Lord, the Liturgy does not express the sense of expectant joy that permeated the Advent season. Nevertheless, the Church does set aside the fourth Sunday in Lent to express our anticipated joy in Christ's Resurrection. This Sunday is called "Laetare Sunday," taken from another Latin word, meaning "rejoice."

The final week of Lent, Holy Week, is particularly important. During this week we concentrate on the events leading up to the Crucifixion of Our Lord. The Gospels that record the Passion of Christ are solemnly read, and the other prayers and readings directly focus on these events.

The season of Lent ends with the solemn announcement of the Resurrection of Our Lord Jesus Christ at the Easter Vigil Mass on Holy Saturday evening. At this Mass we begin our celebration of the feast of Easter and the Easter season. The Easter season is marked by a sense of triumphant joy, since Jesus has overcome death and risen from the dead. This season lasts for fifty days, concluding with the third major feast of the liturgical year, the feast of Pentecost.

Pentecost

Pentecost is the feast that celebrates the presence of the Holy Spirit in the Church. Just as the Holy Spirit spoke through the prophets in the Old Testament, Our Lord promised to his apostles at the Last Supper that he would send the Holy Spirit to guide his Church. ". . . the Holy Spirit . . . will teach you all things and bring to your remembrance all that I have said to you" (Jn 14:26). This promise was ful-

---

Prayer

"It is truly right that with full hearts and minds and voices we should praise the unseen God, the all-powerful Father, and his only Son, Our Lord Jesus Christ."

(Easter proclamation: *Exsultet*)

---

filled on the first Pentecost, and our celebration of this feast reminds us of this great gift.

Ordinary Time

There remains the time in the liturgical year that falls between Christmas and Lent and between Easter and Advent. This time is called ordinary time, since it is not marked by one of the principal events of our faith. "Ordinary," however, does not mean unimportant. This time allows us to reflect more deeply on the mysteries that we have just celebrated and to develop our love for God more fully. Certain Sundays and Holy Days during this time are also set aside to commemorate other significant elements of our faith or events from the life of Our Lord and Our Lady.

The diagram that follows will help us to see these seasons of the year more clearly.

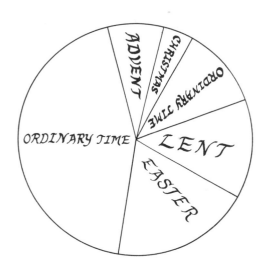

Other Feasts

Now that we have seen the basic framework for the liturgical year, we will fill it in with some of the feasts that occur throughout the year. We can divide these into three main groups: (1) Holy Days, (2) Sunday feasts, and (3) feasts of the saints and Our Blessed Mother. The Church has set aside several days out of the year to commemorate certain significant events in our faith. In the United States, six of these feasts are Holy Days of Obligation, that is, days on which we are obliged to attend Mass. They are: (1) the Immaculate Conception of Our Lady (December 8); (2) Christmas (December 25); (3) the Solemnity of Mary, the Mother of God (January 1); (4) Ascension (forty days after Easter); (5) the Assumption of Our Lady (August 15); and (6) All Saints' Day (November 1). As you can see, these feasts occur throughout the liturgical year, except during the season of Lent.

Several great feasts of the Church are celebrated on Sundays throughout the year. Like the Holy Days, these special Sundays are found throughout the liturgical seasons. During the Christmas season we celebrate the *Feast of the Holy Family*, the model for all families, on the Sunday after Christmas. In the United States the *Feast of the Epiphany* is celebrated on the Sunday closest to January 6. On the following Sunday we celebrate the *Baptism of Jesus*, which marked the beginning of his public life.

In the ordinary time after Pentecost we celebrate two other great mysteries of our faith: the Trinity (on *Trinity Sunday*) and the Eucharist (on the *Feast of Corpus Christi*). Finally, the liturgical year ends with the *Feast of Christ the King*, which reminds us to look ahead to the time when Christ will come in glory and reign as our King.

In addition to Sundays and Holy Days, there are many weekdays throughout the liturgical year that are set aside as special commemorations. Several recall events from the life of Our Blessed Mother. Others honor the saints as great examples of the Christian life. On these days we should call upon Mary and the saints to pray to God on our behalf.

Return to the diagram to see how the feasts fit into the liturgical year. As you have already seen, the colors of the liturgical year change. We see this most clearly in the **vestments**—the special garments worn by the priest and other ministers for celebrating the Liturgy—but also in other decorations in our churches. The three major colors are purple, white, and green. These are used at particular times during the various seasons of the year. *Purple* symbolizes penance and sorrow, so it is used during the seasons of Advent and Lent. *White* symbolizes joy and glory, so it is used at Christmas and Easter. *Green* symbolizes life and hope, so it is used during the ordinary time, when we should be filled with hope.

Three other colors are used less frequently, but also serve to remind us of what we are celebrating. First among these is *red*, which symbolizes fire and blood. It is used on the feast of Pentecost for the Holy Spirit, who was symbolized by fire. It is also used when we celebrate the Passion of Our Lord, the feasts of the martyrs, the feasts of apostles, and the feasts of the evangelists. *Rose* is symbolic of joy in the midst of penance and is used on Laetare and Gaudete Sundays. As we have seen, these Sundays occur during the penitential seasons and are days of rejoicing. Finally, the color *black* is a symbol of mourning. It may be used for Masses for the dead or All Souls' Day.

Thus, we have seen how the Church provides us with a beautiful and meaningful way of worshipping God throughout the year. It enables us to reflect on the key mysteries of our faith and the lives of Our Lord and his Mother as we go from season to season. In order to unite ourselves more perfectly with our fellow Christians, our prayers should reflect the themes so beautifully set forth for us by the Church. Thus, our entire prayer life will become a more perfect form of worship to be given to Almighty God.

Words to Know:

Liturgy   liturgical year   vestments

Church Teaching

"The sacred liturgy is the public worship which Our Redeemer as Head of the Church renders to the Father, as well as the worship which the community of the faithful renders to its Founder and through him to the Heavenly Father. It is, in short, the worship rendered by the Mystical Body of Christ in the entirety of its head and members" (MD).

Q. 65   *What is liturgy?*

Liturgy is the priestly work of Jesus Christ, including the public participation of the People of God in his work. This includes the celebration of the Mass, the other sacraments, and the Liturgy of the Hours (CCC 1069–71).

Q. 66   *What is the liturgical year?*

The liturgical year is the cycle of feasts that surround the life and mysteries of Christ's work on earth. The seasons are Advent and Christmas, Lent and Easter, Pentecost and Ordinary time (CCC 1168–71).

Q. 67   *Why does the Church celebrate feasts of saints and martyrs?*

When the Church celebrates feasts of saints and martyrs, she proclaims the Paschal Mystery in those who have suffered and have been glorified with Christ and raises them up as examples (CCC 1173).

Q. 68   *What is the Liturgy of the Hours?*

The Liturgy of the Hours is the prayer of the Church. It is devised so that the whole course of the day and the night is made holy by the praise of God (CCC 1174–78).

CHAPTER 9

Mary–Mother of the Church

When Jesus saw his mother, and the disciple whom he loved standing near, he said to his mother, "Woman, behold, your son!"

John 19:26

". . . the angel Gabriel was sent from God to a city of Galilee named Nazareth, to a virgin . . . and the virgin's name was Mary. And he came to her and said, 'Hail, full of grace, the Lord is with you! . . . Do not be afraid, Mary, for you have found favor with God. And behold, you will conceive in your womb and bear a son, and you shall call his name Jesus. . . .' And Mary said, 'Behold, I am the handmaid of the Lord; let it be done to me according to your word.' And the angel departed from her" (Lk 1:26–28, 30–31, 38).

These words from St. Luke describe the **Annunciation** and mark the first reference in the Gospels to Mary, the mother of Our Lord. It is appropriate that we should first see her in this scene, since our salvation depends in a great way on this event. Mary was not forced to become the Mother of God. God announced to her through his messenger Gabriel that she had been chosen for this role. Yet his choice required her consent. This consent is beautifully and simply given by Our Lady in her words, "Let it be done to me according to your word."

At the moment of Mary's **fiat** (the Latin word for "let it be done") the "Word became flesh." In other words, the Son of God was conceived in her womb. Mary freely accepted God's will for her and gave life to the Son of God so that we might share in his divine life. Thus, our very salvation depended upon Mary's obedience to the will of God.

The New Eve

Mary's importance for our redemption is reflected in the title frequently given to her by the Fathers of the Church—the "new Eve." Christ has been called the "new Adam," because by his death he undid the harm done by Adam, the first man. So, too, we can speak of Mary and compare her to Eve. "Eve" means "the mother of all the living." Eve helped to bring sin into the world by tempting Adam. Mary, however, helped to bring salvation from sin by listening to and accepting the invitation of God and then becoming the Mother of God. Eve brought death into the world, but Mary brought life—eternal life through Christ. Mary's faith and obedience to God's will correct Eve's pride and disobedience of God's command. Mary, by submitting herself perfectly to God's will, returned to mankind what had been lost to us through original sin.

(Jn 19:26–27). These words were not meant only for Our Lady and St. John, but for all of Jesus' followers. Jesus gave his own Mother to all of us. When Jesus said he would not leave us orphans, he also meant to leave us his Mother. Her care for us is evident in many ways. We call Mary "Our Blessed Mother." Like any mother, Mary has a special love for every one of her children. She leads us into her Son's presence. She watches over each and shares in each one's joys and sorrows. In turning to Mary, as we would to our own mother on earth, we draw closer to God.

In addition to being a spiritual Mother to each of us as individuals, Mary is also the Mother of the whole Church. As Mary was the Mother of Christ's physical body, she is also the Mother of his Mystical Body—the Church —of which we are members through our Baptism.

Mary's role in our redemption goes beyond giving birth to Christ. Her cooperation in God's will began at the Annunciation and continued to the foot of the Cross. There, Mary willingly accepted the death of her Son and joined with him in that suffering. The graces that Christ won for us come to us through Mary. It is for this reason that we can say, "to Jesus, through Mary."

Mary, Our Mother

As Eve was the physical mother of the human race, Mary is our spiritual Mother. While hanging on the Cross, Our Lord spoke to Mary and the apostle John. He said to Mary, "Woman, behold your son!" And then he turned to John and said, "Behold, your mother!"

Privileges Given to Mary

Because Mary was chosen by God to be the Mother of his divine Son, he gave to her several *privileges*. Three of these are: (1) freedom from original sin, (2) complete and per-

---

Prayer

"Mary, Mother of Grace, Mother of Mercy, shield me from the enemy and receive me at the hour of my death."

(Enchiridion, 61)

petual virginity, and (3) freedom from having body and soul separated until the end of the world.

Because Mary was chosen by God to be the Mother of his divine Son, he gave to her several *privileges*. Three of these are: (1) the Immaculate Conception, (2) complete and perpetual virginity, and (3) the Assumption of Mary into heaven, body and soul.

Free from Original Sin: The Immaculate Conception

We know that all human beings have inherited original sin from our first parents, Adam and Eve. When they sinned, they lost for themselves—and for us—the great gift of *sanctifying grace*, God's life in our souls. While we are not personally responsible for original sin, we bear the effects—especially being weak and easily tempted to sin.

Because God wished Mary to be worthy to become the Mother of God, she was created free from all sin, including original sin. God prepared Mary so that she would be worthy to carry the Son of God in her womb. In the same way, the ark of the Covenant was built in the Old Testament to be a fitting receptacle for the written Word of God. God instructed the people, through Moses, that the ark should be built of a rare wood and elaborately decorated with gold. In this way it would be an appropriate symbol of God's presence. How much more fitting was it, then, that God should prepare Mary, who would contain the Word of God himself, not just a symbol of God's presence. Mary is, then, the "new Ark of the Covenant."

Besides Our Lord, Mary is the only human being who was created without original sin. As the poet Wordsworth so beautifully put it, "she is our tainted nature's solitary boast." From the moment of her conception in the womb of her mother, St. Anne, Mary was filled with divine life. Because she was without original sin, she was free from our weakness and inclination to sin. She truly was, as the archangel Gabriel said, "full of grace." This great privilege is called the **Immaculate Conception**.

This doctrine has been taught by the Church but was not formally defined until December 8, 1854, by Pope Pius IX. This was an occasion when papal infallibility was invoked. Our Lady herself confirmed this doctrine four years later. When she appeared to St. Bernadette in the grotto at Lourdes, she identified herself by this title. When asked who she was, Mary replied, "I am the Immaculate Conception."

The feast of the Immaculate Conception, celebrated on December 8, has become a Holy Day of Obligation since the doctrine was defined. This feast is particularly important for Catholics in the United States, for it is under this title that Mary was declared patroness of our country.

Perpetual Virginity

A second great privilege given to Mary was that of **perpetual virginity**. Perpetual virginity means that Mary was always a virgin: before the conception and birth of Christ, during the birth and after the birth of Christ.

While Our Blessed Mother is mentioned only a few times in the Gospels, her virginity is explicitly mentioned by both St. Luke and St. Matthew. In St. Luke's Gospel, Mary tells the angel that she is a virgin. The angel confirms this. In St. Matthew's Gospel, Joseph confirms the fact that he is not the father of the Child in her womb. They are both told that the Child is conceived of the Holy Spirit.

And Mary said to the angel, "How can this be, since I have no husband?" And the angel said to her, "The Holy Spirit will come upon you; therefore the child to be born will be called holy, the Son of God" (Lk 1:34–35).

When his mother Mary had been betrothed to Joseph, before they came together she was found to be with child of the Holy Spirit; . . . an angel of the Lord appeared to him in a dream saying, ". . . that which is conceived in her is of the Holy Spirit . . ." (Mt 1:18, 20).

Mary's virginity is given further testimony in the creeds. In the Apostles' Creed, we proclaim our belief in Jesus Christ, who "was conceived by the power of the Holy Spirit, born of the Virgin Mary. . . ." Similar statements are found in the Nicene Creed, as well as in many other prayers. This doctrine was formally defined at the Second Council of Constantinople in 553 A.D.

Mary's Assumption into Heaven

The third great privilege of Our Lady that we will discuss here is Mary's **Assumption**. The Assumption means that Mary was taken, at the end of her earthly life, body and soul to heaven. When we die, we know that our soul is separated from our body, and so we are not complete. We must wait until the end of the world for God to restore our bodies, in a glorified state, to us. This is one of the consequences that we bear because of original sin. Since Mary was conceived without original sin, it is fitting that God chose to spare the Mother of his Son this consequence of it.

Like the doctrine of the Immaculate Conception, the doctrine of Mary's Assumption has been part of the Church's belief from the beginning. Since about the fifth century, the Eastern rites of the Church have celebrated the feast of the Assumption on August 15. However, it was not until 1950 that this doctrine was formally defined. On November 1 of that year, Pope Pius XII infallibly defined this doctrine. The feast of the Assumption, celebrated on August 15, is now a Holy Day of Obligation.

Mary in Our Lives

"Mary has by grace been exalted above all the angels and men to a place second only to her Son, as the most holy Mother of God who was involved in the mysteries of Christ; she is rightly honored by a special cult in the Church" (LG, 66).

In the Litany of Loreto (see the Appendix), we proclaim Mary as the Queen of angels and the Queen of saints. She has been exalted by God above all other creatures and now holds a place second to her Son, Christ, the King. Why should Mary be placed above even the angels? She has earned this honor because of her role in our salvation and her fullness of grace since the beginning of her life.

Because of Mary's place at the right hand of her Son, she should receive the proper veneration from us. We do not adore Our Lady, since adoration, or divine worship, is reserved for God alone. Rather, we **venerate** her (honor her) above all other creatures because of her special place in our salvation. We believe that she is "full of grace" and as such is "blessed among women." Because of her place, it is fitting, as she herself proclaimed, that "all generations will call [her] blessed" (Lk 1:48).

In honoring Mary we also recognize that she is, as St. Pius X wrote, "our sure way to Christ." As our Mother, Mary will **intercede** in heaven for us, as she did for others when she was on earth. Recall the story of Our Lord's first public miracle. Jesus and his disciples, together with Mary, were at a wedding in Cana. The host ran out of wine, and Mary turned to her Son, asking him to do something about it. And, as we know, Jesus granted her request; he would not refuse his Mother.

This episode teaches us an important lesson. Mary will continue to intercede with Jesus for her children. And Jesus, as he did at Cana, will listen to her pleas for us. Let us remember, then, to turn to Mary in prayer, asking her to give us through her Son the graces we need:

"O Mary, conceived without sin, pray for us, who have recourse to thee."

The Litany of Loreto: Our Lady's Litany

A litany is a form of prayer consisting of a series of petitions, each of which is followed by a fixed response. The litany begins by invoking the Persons of the Trinity and concludes with invocations of the Lamb of God. The body of the litany consists of petitions corresponding to a particular theme. The litanies that are formally recognized by the Church are the litanies to the Holy Name, the Sacred Heart, the Precious Blood, the Blessed Virgin, St. Joseph, and the saints.

The litany of the Blessed Virgin, known as the Litany of Loreto, is a series of invocations of the Blessed Virgin, each with the response, "Pray for us." It contains many beautiful titles of Our Lady and provides us with much to meditate. As you read and say this ancient prayer, which you will find in the Appendix, think about the meaning of each of Mary's titles.

"For behold, henceforth all generations will call me blessed; for he who is mighty has done great things for me. . . ."

(Lk 1:48–49)

Church Teaching

"This motherhood of Mary in the order of grace continues uninterruptedly from the consent which she loyally gave at the Annunciation and which she sustained without wavering beneath the Cross. . . . Taken up to heaven she did not lay aside this saving office but by her manifold intercession continues to bring us the gifts of eternal salvation. By her maternal charity, she cares for the brethren of her Son, who still journey on earth surrounded by dangers and difficulties, until they are led into their blessed home" (*LG*, 62).

LITANY OF THE LORETO

Lord, have mercy on us.
Christ, have mercy on us.
Lord, have mercy on us.
Christ, hear us.
Christ, graciously hear us.
God the Father of heaven,
have mercy on us.
God the Son, Redeemer of the world,
have mercy on us.
God the Holy Spirit,
have mercy on us.
Holy Trinity, One God,
have mercy on us.

Holy Mary, *pray for us.**
Holy Mother of God,
Holy Virgin of virgins,
Mother of Christ,
Mother of divine grace,
Mother most pure,
Mother most chaste,
Mother inviolate,
Mother undefiled,
Mother most amiable,
Mother most admirable,
Mother of good counsel,
Mother of the Church,
Mother of our Creator,
Mother of our Savior,
Virgin most prudent,
Virgin most venerable,
Virgin most renowned,
Virgin most powerful,
Virgin most merciful,
Virgin most faithful,
Mirror of justice,
Seat of wisdom,
Cause of our joy,
Spiritual vessel,
Vessel of honor,
Singular vessel of devotion,
Mystical rose,

*Pray for us is repeated after each invocation.

Tower of David,
Tower of ivory,
House of gold,
Ark of the covenant,
Gate of Heaven,
Morning star,
Health of the sick,
Refuge of sinners,
Comforter of the afflicted,
Help of Christians,
Queen of Angels,
Queen of Patriarchs,
Queen of Prophets,
Queen of Apostles,
Queen of Martyrs,
Queen of Confessors,
Queen of Virgins,
Queen of all Saints,
Queen conceived without original sin,
Queen assumed into heaven,
Queen of the most holy Rosary,
Queen of peace,

Lamb of God, who take away the sins of the world, *spare us, O Lord.*
Lamb of God, who take away the sins of the world, *graciously hear us, O Lord.*
Lamb of God, who take away the sins of the world, *have mercy on us.*

Pray for us, O holy Mother of God.
That we may be made worthy of the promises of Christ.

Let us pray: Grant, we beseech Thee, O Lord God, unto us Thy servants, that we may rejoice in continual health of mind and body; and, by the glorious intercession of blessed Mary ever Virgin, may be delivered from present sadness, and enter into the joy of Thine eternal gladness. Through Christ our Lord. *Amen.*

Words to Know:

Annunciation Fiat Assumption
Immaculate Conception
perpetual virginity venerate intercede

Q. 69 *What is the Immaculate Conception?*

The Immaculate Conception is the gift of God by which Mary was preserved from original sin, from the moment of her conception, by the merits of Jesus Christ (CCC 491).

Q. 70 *What does it mean to say that Jesus was born of the Virgin Mary?*

To say that Jesus was "born of the Virgin Mary" means that by the power of the Holy Spirit, Jesus was conceived in the womb of Mary without a human father (CCC 496, 499).

Q. 71 *What is the Assumption of Mary?*

The Assumption of Mary is a gift from God, given to Mary at the end of her earthly life, whereby she was taken up into heaven body and soul (CCC 966).

Q. 72 *Why is it proper to say that Mary is the Mother of God?*

It is proper to say that Mary is the Mother of God because she is the Mother of Jesus Christ, the Second Person of the Holy Trinity, true God and true Man (CCC 495).

Q. 73 *Do Catholics worship Mary?*

Catholics do not worship Mary, but venerate (honor) her as a model of faith and the greatest of all the saints (CCC 971).

CHAPTER 10

The Communion of Saints

And he who searches the hearts of men knows what is the mind of the Spirit, because the Spirit intercedes for the saints according to the will of God.

Romans 8:27

"Exactly as Christian communion between men on their earthly pilgrimage brings us closer to Christ, so our community with the saints joins us to Christ, from whom, as from its fountain and head, issues all grace and the life of the People of God itself" (LG, 50).

We have seen that the Church is the Mystical Body of Christ with Christ as its head and Mary as its Mother. We who have been baptized in Christ are the members. Membership in the Mystical Body is not limited to those living on earth. Since Baptism leaves us with a permanent character that can never be taken away, those who die faithful to their baptismal promises are still part of the Mystical Body. We use the term **Communion of Saints** to refer to the Church in this sense—as including her members both living and dead.

The term *saint* is used in various ways. In the widest sense, it means "holy one;" all those who have been baptized share in the holiness of Christ. More specifically, saints are those who have died and are with God in heaven. In the strictest sense, the term refers to those who have been officially declared by the Church to be in heaven—those we call the *canonized saints*. The union of these saints is based on our common possession of the life of grace and is expressed through the exchange of spiritual goods. Thus the Communion of Saints includes all of the faithful who are united in Christ—the faithful on earth, the souls in purgatory, and the *blessed*, or saints, in heaven.

The Church Militant

The first part of the Communion of Saints is the faithful on earth. We are known as the **pilgrim Church** since we are journeying (on a pilgrimage) to heaven. Sometimes we also refer to this group as the **Church Militant**. This indicates the "fight," or "struggle," that we on earth must constantly wage against sin and temptation.

Our unity is one of love. We are asked by Christ to carry one another's burdens, to serve each other, to help especially the least among us by the corporal and spiritual works of mercy. This is also done in a special way through prayers for each other. We frequently ask others to pray for us, or we join with them in praying for a particular need.

Intercessory prayer, prayer on behalf of another person, has long been a part of our religious heritage. In the *Old Testament* we often see the leaders and prophets of Israel pray to God for their people. When Our Lord was on earth we heard him pray to his Father for his disciples at the Last Supper. He also encouraged them to pray for one another and for those who would persecute them. In his letters, St. Paul often asks the people to pray for him and mentions his own prayers for them. For example, in his letter to the Christian community in Rome he says ". . . without ceasing I mention you always in my prayers" (Rom 1:9). The Fathers and Doctors of the Church also frequently exhort us to pray for one another. In the Liturgy today the Church encourages us as well. In the *Prayer of the Faithful* at the end of the Liturgy of the Word, we pray expressly for the Church and the needs of her members.

The Church Suffering

Prayer for one another does not end with death. While those in heaven do not need our prayers, those in purgatory do, and we, the Church Militant, can and should pray for them as well. These souls in purgatory represent the second part of the Communion of Saints and are known as the *Church Penitent* or **Church Suffering**.

When we die we do not all necessarily go straight to heaven. Those who do go directly to heaven love God perfectly and have no trace of sin left on their souls. Most of us, however, who die in the state of grace, still have some venial sins on our souls, or may not have sufficiently atoned for past sins, and some punishment due to sin may still be necessary.

The souls in this imperfect state not only need to be cleansed, but they want to be cleansed as well. They know that they are not yet prepared to be in the presence of God. Recalling one of Our Lord's parables may help us understand this:

The Kingdom of heaven may be compared to a king who gave a marriage feast for his son, . . . when the king came in to look at the guests, he saw there a man who had no wedding garment; and he said to him, "Friend, how did you get in here without a wedding garment?" And he was speechless (Mt 22:2, 11–12).

Just as the man who came to the wedding feast was required to have the proper garment, so we must be spotlessly clothed to enter the Kingdom of Heaven. If we are not we will, like the guest at the wedding, be "speechless" before our heavenly King.

Those souls who need to be cleansed and purified before seeing God go to *purgatory*. Purgatory is a place of temporary suffering that cleanses the soul and makes it worthy to see God. The Church's teaching on purgatory is very consoling. Though we are sinful, God in his mercy gives us a chance to make up for these venial sins, and for the punishment still due for our confessed mortal sins. The principal suffering in purgatory is not seeing God. Even though the souls in purgatory really do suffer they are filled with peace because they are assured that they will be with God soon. They no longer fear for their salvation. They know that they are being made ready for heaven.

The souls in purgatory, however, are unable to do anything for themselves to shorten their time there. They depend on us, the Church Militant, to help them. We can do this by offering prayers for them, particularly the Mass, as well as offering other charitable acts. We can also offer our own sufferings here on earth for these souls.

Our Catholic practice of praying for those who have died is rooted in God's revelation to the Jews. In the *Old Testament*, the book of Maccabees tells the story of Judas Maccabeus, who lived in the second century before Christ.

After a battle, it was discovered that some of his dead soldiers who were good men had sinned before their deaths. Judas Maccabeus then had prayers and sacrifices offered to God for these men: ". . . it was a holy and pious thought . . . he made atonement for the dead, that they might be delivered from their sin" (2 Macc 12:45).

In this passage God reveals to us that our prayers can help those who have died. It was also the belief of the early Christians and is part of Tradition. In many ancient Christian tombs we find inscriptions which encourage prayers for those who are buried there.

Because prayer for those who have died is so important, the Church sets aside one day each year on which the whole Church prays for the souls in purgatory. This is All Souls' Day and is celebrated on November 2. The month of November is dedicated to prayers for those who have died, particularly our own family members and friends.

We should not forget the souls in purgatory during the remainder of the year, particularly at Mass, during the Eucharistic prayer when we pray for the dead. But we should try to do this at other times as well. For example, many Catholics add the following short prayer to their prayer before or after meals:

> "May the souls of the faithful departed, through the mercy of God, rest in peace. *Amen*."

There are other things as well that can help us remember to pray for those who have died. Often holy cards are distributed at funerals. The purpose of these cards is to remind us to pray for the person who has died. As pictures in our homes remind us to think of our family members who have died, so, too, these holy cards remind us of them. We should keep them some place where they can remind us to pray for the faithful departed.

The Church Triumphant

The blessed in heaven can also pray for the souls in purgatory, as well as for us on earth. They are the third part of the Communion of Saints—the **Church Triumphant**. Those in the Church Triumphant have completely conquered sin and now share in eternal glory, even before the resurrection of their bodies.

Among the blessed in heaven are the **canonized saints**, whom the Church has officially declared to be in heaven. As we have seen, the most important among these is Our Lady. There are also many other souls who have reached heaven—perhaps some of our own relatives and friends—and deserve to be called saints as well. We do not know for certain who they are, but the Church honors them with a feast each year—the feast of All Saints on November 1.

All these are saints in glory with Christ, who, shining like stars in the firmament, are "standing before the throne and before the Lamb" (Rev 7:9). We are ultimately united with them in our love and union in Christ, and in the grace he gives us. In our prayers, especially in the Liturgy of the Church, we join their heavenly chorus in the glorification of God, saying:

> Blessing and glory and wisdom and thanksgiving and honor and power and might be to our God for ever and ever! *Amen* (Rev 7:12).

We are not just praying alone, each member of the Church by himself. We are united in a community of incomparable grandeur, in a victorious union of love. This great community lifts us up and generates fruits of grace in us.

We partake in this Communion of Saints, and we can turn to the saints for help, just as we turn to other members of the Church on earth. We ask them to intercede with God for us, just as we might ask a friend here to do the same.

We should remember that we are not worshipping the saints, but praying to God *through them*. The saints are truly united with us through Christ and want to help us. St. Thérèse of Lisieux remarked before her death that she would "spend her heaven doing good upon earth." And this is what the saints do when we turn to them.

We are also honoring God when we venerate the saints. The saints are masterpieces of God's grace. Grace has triumphed in them and the devil has been conquered. In venerating them we honor God, whose life shines forth in them.

Devotion to the saints goes back to the early days of the Church. The early Christians began to honor the apostles after their deaths, and later the martyrs were included as well. Gradually, the practice was extended to other holy men and women. The Church recognized their holiness and saw that they could be examples to the faithful. The saints show us that we can reach heaven, and they show us the way.

The saints came from all walks of life—some were married with families, some were priests or religious sisters or brothers, some were kings or queens, some were rich and others poor. Yet, they all had their complete devotion to God in common. Since their lives were so different, it is not surprising that we might find the life of one saint more interesting or helpful to us than another. One often develops a devotion to a particular saint.

For example, the people of one country may have a devotion to a particular saint whose life was intimately connected with their nation. St. Patrick spread the Catholic faith throughout Ireland, and because of this he is the **patron saint** of Ireland. St. Thomas More was a great lawyer and statesman in England. He is the patron saint of all lawyers and also the patron saint of all laypeople because he served God as a layman. We might also have a special devotion to the saint for whom we were named.

Because the lives of the saints are such important examples for us, in the next two chapters we will briefly examine a few of them. This will also give us a chance to see something of the history of the Church as we look at the times in which they lived.

Words to Know:
Communion of Saints   pilgrim Church
Church Militant   intercessory prayer
Church Suffering   Church Triumphant
canonized saint   patron saint

Q. 74 *What does "Communion of Saints" mean?*

The Communion of Saints means that all the faithful, living and dead, share in all the good that exists and is done in the universal Church (CCC 947).

Q. 75 *Do the blessed in heaven and the souls in purgatory form a part of the Communion of Saints?*

The blessed in heaven and the souls in purgatory form a part of the Communion of Saints because they are joined to each other and with us through charity, because those in heaven intercede for us, and those in purgatory gain our assistance by our prayers (CCC 955–58).

Q. 76 *Who are the saints?*

The saints are holy people who are in heaven (CCC 957–58).

Q. 77 *Why should we pray to the saints as well as to God?*

We should pray to the saints as well as to God because God wills to help us through the prayers of others, including the saints, who are very holy and close to him (CCC 956).

Q. 78 *Why are the angels, the saints, and Our Lady powerful intercessors with God?*

The angels, saints, and Our Lady are powerful intercessors with God because they are closely united to Christ in heaven (CCC 956, 2674).

CHAPTER 11

Saints in Our History: The First Thousand Years

For this reason, because I have heard of your faith in the Lord Jesus and your love toward all the saints, I do not cease to give thanks for you, remembering you in my prayers. . . .

Ephesians 1:15–16

About two thousand years have elapsed since the founding of the Church and its birth on Pentecost. As we have seen, it began as a small community, but like the mustard seed in the parable, it has grown and spread throughout the world. During that time it has faced many difficulties and weathered many storms. Yet the Church has survived and is today the same Church of which Our Lord spoke when he said to Peter, ". . . on this rock I will build my church, and the powers of death shall not prevail against it" (Mt 16:18).

The Church could not have survived without the constant guidance and protection of the Holy Spirit. In order to preserve the Church God has raised up many holy men and women who are today recognized as *saints*. With God's help they have been able to put their various talents and personalities in the service of the Church's special need.

The virtuous lives of these saints are still a source of example and inspiration for us today. Let us now look at a few periods in the Church's history as they are reflected in the lives of some of her greatest saints.

"And his gifts were that some should be apostles, some prophets, some evangelists, some pastors and teachers, for the equipment of the saints, for the work of ministry, for building up the body of Christ, until we all attain to the unity of faith and of the knowledge of the Son of God" (Eph 4:11–13).

Apostles and Martyrs

The early days of the Church were marked by the apostles carrying out Our Lord's command: "Go therefore and make disciples of all nations" (Mt 28:19). This *missionary* activity manifests the Church's universality. We have seen that right after Pentecost Peter went out to preach, and by the end of the day three thousand persons were baptized. He was imprisoned, suffered, labored, performed miracles in the name of Jesus, and continued to preach and speak with authority.

Later he went to Antioch and finally to Rome, where he stayed for the rest of his life. Peter thus became the first bishop of Rome.

He was martyred under the Roman Emperor Nero around the year 64 or 67 A.D. It is said that when they were crucifying him Peter said he was not worthy to die as his Master had died, and therefore he asked that the crucifix be turned upside down. He was buried on the Vatican Hill. St. Peter's Basilica was later built over his tomb. Pope St. Linus was elected to succeed him.

The greatest missionary of these early days is the apostle St. Paul. From the time of his conversion, which is described in the Acts of the Apostles, St. Paul preached throughout Palestine, Syria, parts of Asia Minor (modern-day Turkey), Greece, and Rome. During four missionary journeys he zealously preached the good news of Jesus Christ to the Jews and to the **gentiles** (non-Jews). In some places he endured bitter opposition—for example, he was stoned and imprisoned—but still he continued to preach.

In the fourteen letters that he wrote to the communities where he preached, as well as in the accounts of his journeys found in the Acts, we can see St. Paul's great devotion to Christ. Because he so fully carried out Our Lord's command to teach *all* nations, he is called the "Apostle to the Gentiles." Like many of the early Christians, St. Paul not only lived for Christ; around 68 A.D. he died for him as well, as a martyr.

Although the Church continued her missionary work, the next 250 years were characterized by the persecution of Christians. As their numbers increased, and Christianity spread throughout the Roman Empire, the Roman government began to fear the Church. Under certain emperors over the next two centuries, many Christians were put to death for their faith in Christ. Those who died giving witness to their faith were called **martyrs**, the Greek word for witness. Many of them were young and only recently baptized, while still

others had only heard and accepted the message but had not yet been baptized. Yet they all had one thing in common: they willingly accepted horrible tortures and death rather than deny Christ or his message.

These martyrs were an inspiration both to their fellow Christians and to many Roman citizens. In fact, many people were drawn to the faith after seeing those who willingly died for it. They realized that the Christian faith must be great if so many Christians were willing to give up their lives for its sake. The rapid growth of the Church during this period led one early Christian writer to remark that the "blood of the martyrs is the seed of the Church."

Among those whose blood nourished the Church were two young women who lived in the early third century, St. Perpetua and St. Felicity. Perpetua, a young married woman, was from a wealthy family in Carthage, North Africa. Felicity was a young servant in her household. Shortly after Perpetua gave birth to a baby, she and other members of her household, including Felicity, were arrested because they were Christians. Despite her family's pleas that she give up her faith and return home to her child, Perpetua refused and remained strong.

Felicity, who was awaiting the birth of her own child, was eager to join Perpetua in facing death for Christ. The Roman law, however, would not allow a woman who was with child to be put to death. Because Felicity's child was born soon after her imprisonment, she was martyred along with her mistress and the others who had been arrested with them. The willingness of both Perpetua and Felicity to die for Christ—even though they were young women with children they loved—shows us that they placed God first in their lives.

We honor the memories of St. Perpetua and St. Felicity when we ask their intercession during the Eucharistic prayer of the Mass. We also invoke the intercession of many of the other martyrs here. Among them are the first martyr, Stephen; several early popes: Linus, Cletus, Clement, and Sixtus; several holy women: Agatha, Lucy, and Cecilia; and the apostles.

In the same way that the early Christians were inspired by the faith of the martyrs, we too look to them as examples of courage. We also can look to the martyrs of our own times. For although the early centuries of the Church were the age of martyrs, we still have many people who have died—and are dying—for their faith.

Fathers and Doctors of the Church

The great age of martyrdom ended in the early fourth century, when the Roman emperor Constantine issued a decree allowing Christians to practice their religion freely. Once this occurred, Christians were able to preach the gospel in the open. Even though the Church was freed from one problem, she soon had to face others. Trouble now came from within the Church in the form of heresies. A **heresy** is a denial of a basic doctrine of the faith. Those who hold and teach heresies are called *heretics*.

At the time when Constantine became emperor, a major heresy was being preached in Egypt by a priest named Arius. Arius taught that Jesus Christ, the Son of God, was not of the same nature as the Father. In other words, he said that Jesus was not God.

Because Arius was a forceful speaker and persuasive writer, his heresy, called the Arian heresy, spread rapidly through the Church and even deceived many bishops and priests. Because this heresy denied one of the most fundamental doctrines of our faith, it had to be stopped. The first step was the Church council that met in Nicaea in 325 A.D.

One of the bishops who fought to defend the truth during and after that council was **St. Athanasius**. Athanasius was the bishop of Alexandria in Egypt, where he defended the teaching of the Church against many Arian forces. He faced several threats to his life and was exiled for his defense of orthodoxy. Despite all of this, he never wavered in defending the truth that the Son of God is "one in being with the Father."

Many of Athanasius' writings concern the doctrine he defended throughout his life. One of his books, *On the Incarnation*, is a treatise on the mystery of the Second Person of the Trinity made flesh. When he died in 373 A.D., Arianism had not been completely conquered. His efforts, however, were not in vain, and Arianism was finally defeated by 381 A.D.

Other heresies, many of which also concerned the nature of Christ, followed the Arian heresy. Saints were raised up to defend the Church against these heresies as well. One of the greatest saints to defend the Church was

St. Augustine, who was born near the end of Athanasius' life. Although Augustine became a great bishop, teacher, and **theologian** (someone who studies and teaches about God) in the Church, his early life reminds us that even great sinners who repent can become saints.

Born in North Africa, Augustine was the son of a Roman official and a Christian woman named Monica. During his youth he showed that he had a brilliant mind and was recognized as a great student. In his adolescence, however, he acquired many bad habits and lived a wild life; he seriously broke the Commandment on purity. His mother patiently prayed for him, begging God to give him the grace to accept the faith and reform his life.

Her prayers were answered when, after many years of searching for the truth, Augustine was baptized at the age of thirty-three. Later he became a priest and eventually a bishop. During the remainder of his life he preached many sermons and wrote over one hundred books in defense of the faith. Among these books is his own story of his life and his conversion, *The Confessions*. Another book, which many consider his most famous work, is *The City of God*, which contrasts the life of the Christian with the evils of the world in which we must live. Like St. Athanasius, St. Augustine, who died in 430 A.D., is considered one of the Fathers of the Church.

The Monasteries

Later, in the fifth century, barbarian tribes began to threaten the stability of the Roman Empire. The barbarians were warlike, uncivilized tribes living in northern Europe outside the boundaries of the empire. As they expanded, they moved south and began invading the empire, once even threatening the city of Rome. The Church recognized the need to convert them to Christianity and to civilize them.

Much of this work was performed during the next three centuries by the monks. Monks are men who live a life of poverty, chastity, and obedience together in a community in order to serve Christ. They live according to a specific *rule*, or way of life, in communities called **monasteries** that are often in remote areas. They support themselves through agricultural activity and dedicate their time to God. Gradually they formed schools at their monasteries. It was through these schools and their later missionary work that the monks were able to Christianize and educate much of Europe.

Although there were monks in the Church as early as the third century, the title of "Father of Western Monasticism" is given to **St. Benedict**, who was born in 480 A.D. He established the famous monastery at Monte Cassino in Italy and is the founder of the Benedictine order. He composed a rule, which we call the *rule of St. Benedict* to guide the daily activities of his monks.

Benedict divided the daily activities of his monks into prayer and physical work. This became the motto of all Benedictines: "*Ora et Labora*" (pray and work). The daily prayer consisted of the Divine Office—chanted together at seven specific hours of the day and night—and the daily Sacrifice of the Mass. The labor, which was also considered a form of prayer, was both manual—farming, building, and so on—and intellectual—copying of manuscripts, writing books, educating, and the like.

As time passed, the monasteries were not only centers of learning but also missionary centers, from which monks set out to spread the faith. Among these missionary monks was St. Columban, an Irishman who preached the faith among the Franks (living in the area of modern-day France) during the end of the sixth century. Another great example was St. Boniface, a Benedictine monk from England. In the eighth century he left England for the area of Germany. For many years Boniface preached there, spreading the faith and baptizing many from the Germanic tribes.

The Church Faces Problems

While the monks were busy Christianizing the barbarians in Europe, the Church was faced with other invasions as well. A new religion, Islam, had emerged in Arabia early in the seventh century and was now being spread throughout North Africa and the eastern portion of the old Roman Empire. The followers of Islam, called Moslems, eventually gained control of the Mediterranean Sea. As a result, Christians living in western Europe were physically separated from those in the East.

This event intensified problems that had existed for a long time. Christians in the two parts of the empire were divided by language and culture. There had also been a long-running debate over the wording of certain doctrines and over the authority of the bishop of Rome (the Pope). These problems were finally brought to a head in 1054 A.D. In that year, the Church in the East formally separated herself from the Pope and the Roman Catholic Church. This is known as the Eastern *schism*, or split. Schism is a refusal to submit to the Pope or to the Church, which is subject to him. While *some* of the Eastern Christians have been reunited with the Church—for example, the Byzantine Catholics—the schism still exists today.

This schism was only one great problem that the Church faced as she completed her first thousand years. A second was the great corruption of the clergy during part of the *Middle Ages*. This period of increased corruption, from about 850–1000 A.D., was the result of the gradual collapse of the old Roman Empire. As the Empire collapsed, the Church was the only stable force remaining in the world. Because few laymen were educated, it was left to the clergy to take up the responsibility of governing civil society. Many Church leaders then exercised not only spiritual but temporal power as well.

After a while many bishops, priests, and monks began to forget their roles as spiritual leaders. Unfortunately they became far too concerned with their temporal affairs or their own possessions and lost sight of their primary task. Sad to say, there were even popes who, though they never taught error, were sinful, corrupt, and worldly. The need for reform of the clergy became more and more urgent. Once again, many saints rose up during the next few centuries to guide the Church through her next crisis.

Words to Know:

gentiles   martyrs   heresy
St. Athanasius   St. Augustine   St. Benedict
theologian   monasteries

Q. 79   *What is a monastery?*

A monastery is a community of those who consecrate their lives to God through vows of poverty, chastity, and obedience, and who together pray the Liturgy of the Hours (CCC 925, 927).

Q. 80   *What is heresy?*

Heresy is the obstinate denial after Baptism of a truth of the Faith which must be believed (CCC 2089).

Q. 81   *What is schism?*

Schism is a refusal to submit to the Pope or to the Church which is subject to him (CCC 2089).

CHAPTER 12

Saints in Our History: The Second Thousand Years

Having the eyes of your hearts enlightened, that you may know what is the hope to which he has called you, what are the riches of his glorious inheritance in the saints. . . .

Ephesians 1:18

As the Church moved into the eleventh and twelfth centuries, one of her first concerns was reforming the corrupt clergy. Fortunately, the Church was blessed with several holy popes, who were able to begin these reforms.

Other holy men began to reform the monasteries. The most important of these is St. Bernard of Clairvaux. As a young man Bernard joined a new monastic community known as the Cistercians, whose way of life was based on the rule of St. Benedict. But their way of life was simpler and stricter than that in most Benedictine communities of the time.

After he was ordained, Bernard was chosen to begin a new monastery following the Cistercian way of life. Bernard became the abbot of this monastery at Clairvaux and then founded sixty-eight more monasteries according to the same rule. The new generation of monasteries corrected many of the abuses that had crept into monastic life during the Middle Ages, and these monasteries were a great source of hope.

St. Bernard's own holiness was reflected in the life of Clairvaux and the other monasteries. He strengthened the faith by his sermons about devotion to Jesus and to his Mother. So great were these sermons that people from all over Europe came to hear him. Thus St. Bernard was able to rekindle the faith of the laity as well as that of his monks.

The Crusades

St. Bernard had great influence on other matters in Europe as well. For example, he called for the Second Crusade, encouraging many people in France and Germany to join. The **Crusades** were the response of the Church to a new difficulty that had arisen because of the Moslems.

Toward the end of the eleventh century, the Moslems seized control of the *Holy Land* (Palestine) and persecuted those Christians who traveled on pilgrimages to Jerusalem and the other holy places. The Crusades were military efforts to win back the Holy Land. They were carried on periodically during the next two centuries. The knights and soldiers who fought those battles for the cause of Christ used the Cross as their symbol. Many who either led or fought these Crusades were truly saintly men.

One of these courageous men was King St. Louis IX of France, who led the last two major Crusades. He is noted for being a holy man and a just ruler. His devotion to his faith was instilled in him at an early age by his mother. When he was growing up she often said to him, "I love you, my dear son, as much as a mother can love her child, but I would rather see you dead at my feet than that you should commit a mortal sin." Such lessons never left him, even when he became the king of France.

While he was king, he attended two Masses each day and spent much of his time in prayer. He frequently cared for the poor personally, often having them join his family at meals. And he taught his sons to love their faith as well. In his last words to his eldest son he wrote, ". . . the first thing I would teach thee is to set thine heart to love God."

For St. Louis, as for any saint, love of God came first. Thus, when it seemed necessary to fight a battle for Christ, St. Louis readily responded. He died on his way to fight his second Crusade. His last words echoed those of Our Lord on the Cross, "Into thy hands I commend my spirit."

Despite their great efforts, the Crusaders did not finally achieve their goal. The Holy Land was not freed from the Moslems. The Crusades did, however, strengthen the faith of many in Europe and increase devotion to Christ and his saints. They also opened western Europe to many areas of knowledge in which the Moslems had advanced—for example, navigation, medicine, and philosophy. This provided the basis for many scholarly and scientific achievements during the next few centuries.

The internal reforms of the Church, begun by St. Bernard and others, grew and flourished during the thirteenth century. This was the height of the period known as the **Middle Ages**.

New Religious Orders

During this century, two new religious orders were founded that were dramatically different from the traditional orders. The members of these communities did not live in monasteries isolated from society but lived instead in the towns where they worked. Unlike the monastic communities, which owned large portions of land to support themselves, these new orders depended on the generosity of ordinary people for their basic needs. They are called *mendicant* orders, because they lived by begging. By living simply, these orders reminded Christians that the true role of the religious was to serve God.

The first of these communities was the Franciscan order, which was founded in Italy by **St. Francis of Assisi**. Francis, the son of a wealthy merchant in Assisi, grew up with plenty of money, which he spent recklessly. He wanted to become a knight but realized that Christ was calling him to serve God in the religious life. Francis then decided to live as a poor man, discarding his fine clothes for those of a beggar and caring for the needy and the sick.

He began a life of prayer—preaching and serving the poor. His holiness attracted many young men, who joined him in his work. Eventually Francis wrote a simple rule for his followers. With the Pope's blessing they were established as the Order of Friars Minor ("Little Brothers"). By the time of Francis' death, there were over five thousand Franciscans in Europe.

Men were not the only ones attracted to Francis' way of life. A rich young woman from Assisi also asked to join him, and thus with Francis' help St. Clare established a community for women, the Poor Clares, who also lived according to the Franciscan rule.

Another mendicant order for men was founded by a young Spanish priest, Dominic de Guzman. This order is known as the Dominicans, or Order of Preachers. As a young priest **St. Dominic** was sent to convert a group of heretics living in southern France, the Albigensians. To help him in this task, he gathered a group of young men who were willing to dedicate themselves to preaching. Like the Franciscans, they lived in simplicity and poverty. They spent their time in teaching and preaching. The Dominicans emphasized scholarly learning for their members, so that they would be able to preach more effectively. Consequently, many of the great university teachers of this age were Dominicans.

St. Thomas Aquinas

The greatest of these Dominican scholars and teachers was **St. Thomas Aquinas**. Thomas was born in Italy in 1225 A.D. and began his education at the Benedictine monastery at Monte Cassino. His wealthy family hoped that one day he would become a Benedictine. Thomas went on to study at the University of Naples, where he first met the Dominicans. Their simple life of poverty and study attracted Thomas, and, despite many vigorous objections from his family, he joined the order.

He studied theology and philosophy with another Dominican, St. Albert the Great, and eventually became a teacher himself at the University of Paris.

Thomas studied the ancient Greek philosopher Aristotle, whose writings were among those brought back to Europe by the Crusaders. St. Thomas used Aristotle's ideas in his own work in theology. He taught that God's revelation to man is not contrary to reason but, rather, that reason is necessary to understand God more completely. While his method was based on Aristotle, his insights were based on the Scriptures and the writings of the Fathers. He wrote a large number of books, but the best known and most important of these is his *Summa Theologiae*. In this famous book he organized, explained, and defended all the doctrines of our faith. Thomas' writings have never been surpassed in the Church and remain today among the most important sources for Catholic theology.

Although Thomas' scholarly works were important to the Church, it was his love of God that made him a saint. His devotion to Christ and the Blessed Sacrament are reflected in some of the beautiful prayers and poems he composed for certain feasts. For example, St. Thomas wrote the beautiful hymn *Pange Lingua* ("Sing My Tongue"), the final verses of which are frequently sung at Benediction. Christ and the Church were the center of St. Thomas' life, and he knew that his writings were unimportant compared to the infinite wisdom of God.

In 1274 A.D. St. Thomas was asked by the Pope to attend the Church council in Lyons,

France. While on his way he became ill and died on March 7, 1274. Before he died, he displayed his humility and love for God. As he prepared to receive the Eucharist for the last time, he said:

I receive thee, price of my redemption, Viaticum of my pilgrimage, for love of whom I have fasted, prayed, taught, and labored. Never have I said a word against thee. If I have it was in ignorance and I do not persist in my ignorance. I leave the correction of my work to the Holy Catholic Church, and in that obedience I pass from this life.

St. Catherine of Siena

Although the Church flourished in the thirteenth century, she suffered many problems in the centuries that followed. During the fourteenth century debates between the popes and the kings of France created a major crisis. For the first time since St. Peter, the Pope was not in Rome. For seventy years the popes lived in the French city of Avignon. It was a woman from Siena, Italy, who finally persuaded the Pope that he must return to Rome.

St. Catherine of Siena was a young laywoman who had chosen to live a life of prayer and service to others, particularly the sick. Her reputation for holiness spread throughout Italy, and many people turned to her for help and advice.

Several times Catherine went to Pope Gregory XI, urging him to return to Rome for the good of the Church. Finally, she visited him in Avignon, pointing out to him that many of the Church's problems stemmed from the absence of the popes from Rome. Pope Gregory listened to her, returned to Rome, and began to reform the Church. Catherine died only a few years later at the age of thirty-three. Because of her many spiritual writings, Catherine was declared a Doctor of the Church.

Although St. Catherine helped the Church end one crisis, another, even greater, followed almost immediately. For the next forty years there were two men, one in Avignon and one in Rome, who claimed to be Pope. This confusion, known as the **Great Western Schism**, divided the Church and weakened the role of the Pope. By the time it was resolved, the Church's unity was threatened.

Protestant Reformation

The fifteenth century also brought with it many new developments. This age is known as the **Renaissance** (rebirth) because of the renewed interest in the ancient Greek and Roman civilizations. During this time many of the clergy were once again corrupted by money and other luxuries. Also, the invention of the printing press made it possible for new ideas —some heretical—to spread more rapidly. By the beginning of the sixteenth century, the Church was once more in need of reform.

teaching young women, were formed by St. Angela Merici. The most important of these new communities was the Society of Jesus (the Jesuits), founded by *St. Ignatius of Loyola*.

St. Ignatius of Loyola

St. Ignatius of Loyola was a Spanish nobleman who was trained to be a soldier. During his career, he became noted for his bravery and loyalty to his king. In one battle he was seriously wounded and required several months of rest. During this time he read the only books that were available to him—a life of Christ and some lives of the saints. By the time his leg had healed, his life had changed. St. Ignatius vowed to become a "soldier" in the service of Christ and his Church.

After a time of spiritual retreat, Ignatius began to study theology to prepare himself for his new work. While he was studying at the University of Paris, he was joined by other young men, and together they made their first vows of poverty and chastity. After a few years they formed themselves into an order and offered their services to the Pope.

The special work of the Society of Jesus was to defend the faith and serve the Church in whatever way or place the Pope asked them. At the beginning this took the form of defending the faith against the attacks of the Protestants. For example, many Jesuits were sent to Germany to preach against Lutheranism, and they were successful in bringing many people back to the Church. As time passed, the Society began to establish its own universities, convinced that a strong Catholic education would ensure loyalty to the Church.

The motto of St. Ignatius and his Society is "*Ad Majorem Dei Gloriam*" ("to the greater glory of God"). He really lived only for God's glory, and that eventually made him a saint.

Unfortunately, some attempts to reform the Church led the "reformers" away from her. This is known as the **Protestant Reformation**. Beginning with Martin Luther, several groups rebelled and broke away from the Church. This was the beginning of the many Christian denominations we see around us today.

This tremendous upheaval was the reason that the Church called the Council of Trent. The Church did need reform, and she also needed to clarify the doctrines that were being challenged by the Protestants. The work of this council strengthened the Church so that she emerged from her latest crisis stronger and more able to face the work ahead.

The period immediately following the council is known as the **Counter-Reformation**. Just as new religious orders had helped the Church to reform during the Middle Ages, likewise new religious orders helped the Church to renew herself at this time. For example, the Ursuline sisters, dedicated to

Missionaries to the New World

In the centuries that followed, the Church, strong and healthy once more, began to spread even further. The European nations had begun to explore and colonize territories in Asia, Africa, and the Americas. The Church also was active, spreading the faith to the people in these areas. The greatest missionary activity since the early days of the Church followed the Reformation.

One of the greatest missionaries at this time was a Jesuit, St. Francis Xavier. He was among the original members of the Society of Jesus and was chosen by St. Ignatius to be one of the Society's first missionaries. Like the great missionary St. Paul, Francis covered a vast territory in a very short time.

His preaching began in India. From there he traveled through Sri Lanka, Malaysia (Indonesia), and Japan, converting many as he went. He died before he could enter China, but future Jesuits, Franciscans, and Dominicans who continued his work did preach the gospel in China. The work begun by St. Francis Xavier paved the way for later missionaries to the Orient.

Jesuit missionaries from France were among those who brought the message of Christ to the French territories in North America. St. Isaac Jogues and seven others are called the "North American martyrs." They preached among the Indians and suffered martyrdom for their faith.

Spanish missionaries labored in the southwestern and western portions of the North American continent. One of the most notable is the Franciscan priest Fr. Junipero Serra, who founded a series of missions among the Indians in California.

With the work of the missionaries and Catholics who settled in America from Europe, the faith was planted on American soil. The first saint born in the United States was St. Elizabeth Ann Seton, who was born in 1774.

Elizabeth was raised as an Episcopalian and married William Seton, a prosperous merchant from New York. They had five children. When Elizabeth's husband became ill with tuberculosis, they moved to Italy, where he died. In Italy Elizabeth became convinced that the Roman Catholic Church was the true Church.

When she returned home, Elizabeth became a Catholic, despite the strong objections of her family and friends. To support herself and her children she opened a school for other young children in her vicinity and later in Maryland. Her school was unusual because it was intended for any student, not just the children of the rich. This was the beginning of the Catholic school system in the United States.

Other young women joined her. In time this group became a religious community, the Sisters of Charity. Founded in 1809, this was the first religious order to be founded in America.

During this time of missionary expansion, the Church was challenged by the scientific, intellectual, and political revolutions taking place in Europe. The Church was constantly called upon to defend herself but was able to remain strong.

Modern Times

As the Church entered the twentieth century, she was blessed with a saintly Pope, Pius X. A simple country priest, but also a great teacher, Pius was able to help the Church face one of the greatest heresies in her history—**Modernism**. Modernists think that teachings on faith and morals should change and evolve, and that there is no unchangeable, objective revelation from God on which Christianity is based. In addition, modernists deny the reality of supernatural events, such as miracles, which support the Christian faith. Pope Pius X wrote two great encyclicals summarizing and refuting these ideas.

Pope St. Pius served as a great shepherd of the Church. He encouraged frequent reception of Holy Communion. He reminded Catholics that the Eucharist is our spiritual food. He also lowered the age at which young children may first receive this great sacrament. In addition, Pope Pius X encouraged the Catholic laity to become involved in charitable work among the poor. He died broken hearted as the First World War began, expressing his simplicity in his last will and testament, "I was born poor, I lived poor, I die poor."

Since his death, the Church and the world have faced more challenges—particularly the spread of *atheistic, totalitarian* forms of government in various nations. The two world wars since the death of Pius X remind us of the terrible evils of *Nazism, communism*, and *fascism*. In opposition to these evils, one of the great saints of this century, St. Maximilian Kolbe, shines forth as an example for our times.

Maximilian was born in Poland near the turn of the century. As a member of the Franciscan order, he devoted much of his time and intelligence to understanding the role of Our Lady in our salvation. Before he was ordained, he organized a group of the friars into what he called the "Knights of Mary Immaculate." Members of this group dedicated themselves to win the whole world for Mary. After his ordination, he also gathered lay people into his group. In order to spread his message further, in the early 1920s he began a magazine called *The Knight of the Immaculate*. He had no financial backing, but the magazine thrived surprisingly, although it continually faced financial difficulties. He also established a community in Nagasaki, Japan, which later miraculously survived the atom bomb.

In 1936, after establishing the community in Japan, Maximilian returned to Poland. At this time Hitler came to power in Germany, and soon his armies invaded Poland. Maximilian was arrested by the Gestapo and imprisoned in Auschwitz in 1941.

Maximilian was immediately a source of strength for all imprisoned with him. Shortly after he arrived, some prisoners escaped from the camp. In retaliation, the Nazis randomly chose ten prisoners to be starved to death. One man who was chosen, Sgt. Francis Gajowniczek, began to cry for his wife and children. At this point Fr. Maximilian asked the guards if he could take the sergeant's place. When asked why he chose to do this, he answered, "I am a Catholic priest." With that Maximilian Kolbe began the road to his martyrdom. He prayed and gave courage to the other nine men in the starvation bunker. To the complete surprise of the Nazi guards, he was still alive after three weeks of neither food nor water, and they finally killed him. St. Maximilian died as he had lived—offering his life to God.

In our times the Church continues to grow, as the faith is spread in places such as India and Africa. After two thousand years we see that the Holy Spirit continues to guide the Church. Christ's promise continues: ". . . the powers of death shall not prevail against it."

Words to Know:

Crusades   Middle Ages
St. Francis of Assisi
St. Dominic   St. Thomas Aquinas
St. Catherine of Siena
Great Western Schism   Renaissance
Protestant Reformation
Counter-Reformation
St. Ignatius of Loyola   Modernism

Q. 82   *What is a mendicant order?*
A mendicant order is a religious community which relies on the generosity of others for its basic needs (CCC 927).

Q. 83   *What is a Protestant?*
A Protestant is a Christian who belongs to a church which separated from the Catholic Church in the sixteenth century (CCC 838).

St. Dominic receiving the Rosary from Our Lady.

"Exactly as Christian communion between men on their earthly pilgrimage brings us closer to Christ, so our community with the saints joins us to Christ, from whom as from its fountain and head issues all grace and the life of the People of God itself."

(LG, 50)

CHAPTER 13

Separated Brethren

"I do not pray for these only, but also for those who believe in me through their word, that they may all be one; even as thou, Father, art in me, and I in thee, that they also may be in us, so that the world may believe that thou hast sent me."

John 17:20–21

The universality of the Church is manifested in our times by the millions of Catholics throughout the world. At the same time, there are still many people who do not belong to the Catholic Church yet are members of various organized religions. Of these people, some believe in Christ, while others do not, even though they believe in the one, true God. There are others who may have some sort of religion but do not believe in the one, true God. All of these people are outside the visible Church, but in varying degrees. In this chapter we will consider their relationship to the Church.

> Let us pray for all our brothers and sisters who share our faith in Jesus Christ, that God may gather and keep together in one Church all those who seek the truth with sincerity *(General Intercession from the Liturgy of Good Friday).*

Those closest to the Church are non-Catholic Christians who have been baptized. They are often referred to as our **separated brethren**. They are united in some way to the Mystical Body in virtue of their Baptism. This is because there is but "one Baptism for the forgiveness of sins," as we profess in the Nicene Creed. We are all baptized in Christ. Thus anyone who has received the Sacrament of Baptism has been united to Christ and his Body, the Church. Such a person is put in a certain, although imperfect communion with the Catholic Church.

What divides Christians, however, is the degree to which they possess the teachings and practices handed down through the apostles from Christ. Many elements of truth and holiness exist outside the visible structure of the Catholic Church. These elements include the Bible, the life of grace, and the gifts of faith, hope, and charity. The Holy Spirit uses these elements possessed by non-Catholic churches and communities to bring people to salvation. Christ gives all these gifts of truth and grace to the Catholic Church. These gifts come from Christ and help people to unity in the Catholic Church. At the same time, it is only the Catholic Church that teaches the full message of Our Lord. The divisions in belief and practice among Christians vary by degrees. Those who are closest to the Church are the Orthodox Christians, who possess all of the sacraments but who have separated themselves from the authority of the Church. They did this, as we saw, one thousand years ago when they rejected the authority of the Pope.

In the next place are those denominations that broke away from the Church at the time of the Reformation—for example, the Lutherans. In addition to separating themselves from the authority of the Church, these groups also rejected certain teachings and sacraments of the Church. The Lutherans, for example, rejected the need for the Sacrament of Penance and taught that individuals may interpret the Scriptures without the guidance of the Church.

Finally, there are Christian denominations that have broken from these groups, rejecting still more doctrines of our faith. Since the Reformation, new Christian denominations have continued to appear, as people decided to keep certain parts of the message of Christ while rejecting others.

While all of these various Christian groups possess some parts of Christ's gospel, they are still separated from the fullness of his message.

The fullness of unity in the Church requires that all Christians be united again in doctrine and worship. The Church prays for this, especially in the Liturgy of Good Friday. The message of the prayer is that those united to Christ, initially in Baptism, may be fully united with him in faith.

Almighty and eternal God, long ago you gave your promise to Abraham and his posterity. Listen to your Church as we pray that the people you first made your own may arrive at the fullness of redemption *(General Intercession from the Liturgy of Good Friday)*.

Then there are those people who do not believe in Christ, but who do believe in the one, true God. These are the Jews and the Moslems. The Jews, by virtue of their history, bear a closer relationship with the Church.

The Jews were the first **chosen people**. God first revealed himself to man when he made the Covenant with Abraham. He promised that Abraham's descendants would be his special people and that he would be their God.

Over the centuries God gradually revealed himself to these people, preparing them specially for his spiritual Kingdom, which was still to come. God revealed to his people that salvation would come to the world through them. God promised that he would restore to the world the harmony and closeness to God that had existed before the Fall. This would be accomplished by a descendant of Abraham—the Messiah.

When they had been instructed and formed, the Jews were ready to receive the fullness of God's revelation. They were ready to be transformed into the wholly spiritual people God had intended them to be. And so Jesus Christ, the Son of God, came into the world.

Many of the Jews, however, did not recognize him as the Messiah. Because of this, they are separated from the Church today. They should be members of the Church, for salvation came from them. Jesus himself said to the Samaritan woman at the well, "salvation comes from the Jews" (Jn 4:22). A special bond unites us with them. Jesus sprang from their own stock; he was "Son of David." God still loves them with a special love. We pray that they may recognize in Our Lord their own Messiah promised by God—and thus once more become part of the new People of God, as they had been destined to be.

Like the Jews, the Moslems also believe in the one, true God of Creation. However, unlike Judaism, their religion is not the preparation for Christianity. The Moslem religion—Islam—developed in Arabia about six hundred years after Christ and draws from both Judaism and

Christianity. They accept some of the revelation of God to the Jews found in the Old Testament but do not recognize Christ as the Son of God. They see him as one of the prophets, not as the Second Person of the Trinity. We pray that the Moslems, too, may see the truth and one day be fully united to the Church.

> Almighty and eternal God, you created mankind so that all might long to find you and have peace when you are found. Grant that, in spite of hurtful things that stand in their way, they may all recognize in the lives of Christians the tokens of your love and mercy and gladly acknowledge you as the one true God and Father of us all *(General Intercession from the Liturgy of Good Friday)*.

Then there are those people—both the *pagans* and the *atheists*—who do not believe in the one, true God at all. The pagans are those who do not believe in the only true God but may practice some form of idolatrous religion or even believe in many gods, which is called **polytheism**. The ancient Greek and Roman religions were of this sort. There are also those pagans who practice **animism**, believing that inanimate objects possess supernatural powers and can be controlled by us. The pagans then worship many gods, but not the one, true God.

There are also people who are **atheists**. Strictly speaking, atheism is the denial of the existence of a personal God. In our modern world atheism takes many forms. There are those who expressly deny God's existence. Others maintain that there may be a God but that we can know nothing about him. We call these people **agnostics**. Still other people do not expressly deny God's existence but never take any interest in God or religion. They choose to ignore him and concentrate on mankind and its accomplishments instead.

There can be many obstacles that prevent these people from believing in God. We pray that God will remove these obstacles, so they too may come to believe in him.

As members of the Church we should work toward the reunion of all Christians with the Church and pray that all others outside the Church might fully become members of the Mystical Body. This is what is meant by **ecumenism**. As Catholics we have been given a great gift, and we should have a longing to share this gift with others.

We know that salvation has come into the world through Christ. He left us the Church to distribute to us the graces of salvation and to provide a secure guide for us. We have been blessed with the sacraments that help us on our path to heaven. Christ also left us with a visible representative on earth, so that we might clearly see his message in the world. Those who are outside the Catholic Church do not have these great gifts. Does this mean, then, that those who are outside the visible Church cannot be saved?

The Church teaches that "outside the Catholic Church there is no salvation." What exactly does this mean? The Church is necessary for salvation because Jesus Christ is necessary for

". . . it is through Christ's Catholic Church alone, which is the universal help towards salvation, that the fullness of the means of salvation can be obtained" (UR, 3).

salvation. Jesus and his message are found completely in the Church—his Body.

The Church does not teach, however, that all of those who are outside the visible Church will not be saved. Only those who know that God wants them to be in full communion with the Catholic Church, yet who deliberately choose to remain outside the Church—by willingly rejecting Christ and his message—will not be saved. There are many people, though, who are outside the visible Church through no fault of their own. For example, there are many who have never heard the gospel or may have a distorted picture of it. Even so, lack of the gospel or the fullness of the gospel does not mean that these people are without the grace necessary for salvation. If they seek God with a sincere heart, and moved by grace try to do God's will as they understand it through their consciences, they have the hope of salvation.

But a problem still exists. Our Lord told us that Baptism *is* necessary in order to enter heaven. When he spoke to the Pharisee Nicodemus, he said:

Truly, truly I say to you, unless one is born of water and the Spirit, he cannot enter the kingdom of God (Jn 3:5).

We have already seen that those Christians who are outside the Church are truly baptized in Christ, but what about those who have never been baptized—can they enter into the Kingdom of God?

For those who do not know of the sacrament and its importance, or who are unable to receive it before they die, there are two other means of receiving the sanctifying grace necessary to enter heaven. The first is called *Baptism of desire*. This desire for Baptism can be explicit as in the case of someone who is preparing for Baptism but who dies before receiving the sacrament. Or it can be implicit. The desire is implied in those people who *faithfully* and *truly* try to carry out God's will in their lives. Perhaps they do not know of the need for Baptism but would receive it if they did. God, knowing their thoughts and desires, does not punish them for circumstances beyond their control.

The second extraordinary means of receiving the grace necessary for heaven is called *Baptism of blood*. This is the "baptism" granted to those non-Christians who have been martyred for Christ. The fact that they are willing to die for Christ demonstrates their faith and love, and they are welcomed into heaven, even though they have never received sacramental Baptism.

Now that we see the great gift we have been given by being baptized and raised as members of the Catholic Church, we should work to bring others into union with the Church. At the same time we should show respect for the religions of others, leading them with patience and compassion to see the fullness of truth.

We ought to see that we are unworthy to receive such a gift, and not think that this entitles us to feel smug and superior. Indeed we

"I, therefore, a prisoner for the Lord, beg you to lead a life worthy of the calling to which you have been called, with all lowliness and meekness, with patience, forbearing one another in love, eager to maintain the unity of the Spirit in the bond of peace."

(Eph 4:1–3)

can learn from so many of our separated brethren.

The Eastern Orthodox venerate tradition. The splendor of their liturgy inspires in us deep reverence for the worship of God. Episcopalians have a great understanding for the beauty of ceremonies. Lutherans, Baptists, and Evangelicals read the Bible and are very familiar with it. Jews have a deep sense of the sacred, love of the Commandments, and the courage to stand up for their beliefs.

We Catholics must live our faith more seriously. Our love must increase, and each of us must personally convert, turn away from sinful ways, and follow Christ.

Words to Know:
separated brethren   chosen people   polytheism   animism   atheists   agnostic   ecumenism

---

Church Teaching

"For although the Catholic Church has been endowed with all divinely revealed truth and with all means of grace, yet her members fail to live by them with all the fervor that they should. As a result the radiance of the Church's face shines less brightly in the eyes of our separated brethren and of the world at large, and the growth of God's Kingdom is retarded. Every Catholic must therefore aim at Christian perfection and, each according to his station, play his part, that the Church, which bears in her own body the humility and dying of Jesus, may daily be more purified and renewed, against the day when Christ will present her to himself in all her glory without spot or wrinkle" (UR, 4).

Q. 84 *Can another church, outside the Catholic Church, be the Church of Christ?*

No church outside the Catholic Church can be the Church of Christ, although other churches can be imperfectly united with the Church of Christ, which exists fully in the Catholic Church alone (CCC 816, 838).

Q. 85 *Is it a serious loss to be outside the Church?*

It is a most serious loss to be outside the Church, because outside one does not have either the means, which have been established, or the secure guidance, which has been set up for eternal salvation, which is the only thing truly necessary for man (CCC 846–48).

PART TWO
The Christian
In the World

96

CHAPTER 14

The Universal Call to Holiness

You, therefore, must be perfect, as your heavenly Father is perfect.

Matthew 5:48

As members of the Mystical Body we have a general calling, or **vocation**, from God. Each Christian is called to **holiness**, which means that we are each called to follow Christ so that one day we may be with him in heaven for eternity. As St. Paul tells us in his letter to the Christians in Ephesus, God "chose us in him before the foundation of the world, that we should be holy and blameless before him" (Eph 1:4). The vocation of each Christian, then, is to become a saint.

In addition to becoming saints, we are also called by God to spread the faith given at our Baptism. Each of us must be a missionary, or apostle, for Christ, preaching the gospel in whatever way we can, by word and by example. We call this work the **apostolate**.

For each of us, becoming a saint and spreading the faith are done in different ways. This is our *specific vocation*, to which God calls us, according to our own gifts, talents, and circumstances. St. Paul, in his letter to the Romans, reminds us that the Church, like the body, has many members, each of which has its own particular role:

Having gifts that differ according to the grace given to us, let us use them: if prophecy, in proportion to our faith; if service, in our serving; he who teaches, in his teaching; he who exhorts, in his exhortation; he who contributes, in liberality; he who gives aid, with zeal; he who does acts of mercy, with cheerfulness (Rom 12:6–8).

Thus our own particular vocation depends upon the gifts that God has given us.

In discovering our vocation, we cannot simply follow our own desires, for often these may lead us away from God. Nor can we expect God to hand us a detailed list of instructions about how to live our lives. Rather, we should pray for the wisdom to recognize our talents and abilities—as well as our limitations—and to choose our life's work accordingly. We also have to recognize the circumstances we are in, where God has placed us. For instance, a father who has to take care of his family cannot say, "Well, I have a special gift to be an artist [or some other talent], so I ought to pursue that instead of the drudgery of my job or the care of my children." In later chapters we will consider the possible states of life to which God may call us.

Obstacles to Holiness

Before considering how to become holy, we shall look first at those things that are obstacles to holiness. We know that all men are born with original sin, and that it is removed through Baptism. After Baptism, however, we are still weak and inclined toward sin. We are still easily tempted, and inclined toward evil, toward disobedience to God and his Commandments.

This inclination to sin can also be seen in the way we often use our natural tendencies. God has placed in all men certain tendencies to help us live here on earth. For example, we have a natural desire for food and drink so that we can survive physically. Because of original sin it is easy for these tendencies to get out of control. When this occurs, they lead us to sin. For example, the desire for food and drink can become excessive, leading a person to gluttony or drunkenness.

If we allow these tendencies to get out of control frequently, they can become *habits*. A **habit** is a way of acting that is acquired by repetition of certain actions. Habits are a familiar part of our daily routine. We brush our teeth, for example, without giving it much thought. Once we have learned to ride a bicycle, we develop the habit and ride without thinking about all the steps we are following. These habits are morally indifferent—that is, they are neither good nor evil. Some habits, however, are sinful. These are acquired by repeatedly doing bad actions and are known as vices.

There are seven principal vices, which are known as the seven **capital sins**. They are called *capital*, from the Latin word for head or source, because they are the source of all other sins and vices. They are not the only vices, just the chief ones from which many more stem. Because these vices are the major obstacles in our path to holiness, we should consider each of them briefly and learn to recognize them.

> *"The beginning of man's pride is to depart from the Lord. . . . For the beginning of pride is sin, and the man who clings to it pours out abominations" (Sir 10:12–13).*

Pride is the chief capital sin, for it is at the root of all the others. It is an *excessive, disordered* love of oneself. This leads us to prefer our own desires to those of God and our neigh-

---

Church Teaching

"It is therefore quite clear that all Christians in any state or walk of life are called to the fullness of Christian life and to the perfection of love, and by this holiness a more human manner of life is fostered also in earthly society. In order to reach this perfection the faithful should use the strength dealt out to them by Christ's gift, so that, following in his footsteps and conformed to his image, doing the will of God in everything, they may wholeheartedly devote themselves to the glory of God and to the service of their neighbor" (LG, 40).

bors. It is pride that was at the root of the sin of our first parents—their desire to be like God. They did not want to be subordinate, as creatures, to their Creator. We should not confuse this vice with the rightful pride we take in our accomplishments or with a correct sense of self-esteem. These are sinful only if we exaggerate them.

> *"And [Jesus] said to them, 'Take heed, and beware of all covetousness; for a man's life does not consist in the abundance of his possessions' " (Lk 12:15).*

Covetousness, or avarice, means greed. It is an uncontrolled desire for earthly possessions, such as money, clothes, and so on. A certain desire for these things is natural, since they are necessary in order to live in the world. However, we must constantly take care that these desires do not turn to greed, and that we do not put these things first in our lives or ahead of more important values. Not only is covetousness itself wrong, as the Ninth and Tenth Commandments tell us, but greed can easily lead to further sins. For example, the person with this vice may eventually lie, cheat, steal, or even murder, in order to possess those things he desires.

> *"But I say, walk by the Spirit, and do not gratify the desires of the flesh. For the desires of the flesh are against the Spirit, and the desires of the Spirit are against the flesh; . . . Now the works of the flesh are plain: immorality, impurity, licentiousness" (Gal 5:16–17, 19).*

Lust is the uncontrolled desire for or indulgence in sexual pleasure. It should not be confused with the lawful use of our sexual powers within the holy state of marriage. God created human beings with a natural attraction to the opposite sex. As long as this attraction is controlled and ordered finally to Christian mar-

riage, it is healthy and good. This attraction becomes disordered when it is focused on our own pleasure instead of a selfless, true love of another person, and when it is separated from marriage and the purpose of marriage.

> *"Be angry but do not sin; do not let the sun go down on your anger. . . . Let all bitterness and wrath and anger and clamor and slander be put away from you" (Eph 4:26, 31).*

Anger is an uncontrolled expression of displeasure and antagonism, often accompanied by a desire for revenge. This is not the same as the righteous anger spoken of by St. Paul in his letter to the Ephesians or that exhibited by Our Lord when he threw the moneychangers out of the Temple. Anger is the proper response to an injustice—for example, defrauding the poor or abortion—but we must control it and use it properly. If our anger is uncontrolled or if it is bitter and full of hate and we seek only revenge, it has become a vice.

"Let your light so shine before men, that they may see your good works and give glory to your Father who is in heaven."

(Matthew 5:16)

"Do not have an insatiable appetite for any luxury, and do not give yourself up to food; . . . Many have died of gluttony, but he who is careful to avoid it prolongs his life" (Sir 37:29–31).

Gluttony is an uncontrolled desire for and indulgence in food and drink. Eating and drinking are intended to be pleasurable and are certainly not sinful in themselves. In fact, they are necessary for our survival. However, like our desire for possessions, these desires can become excessive and be abused by us.

"For where jealousy [envy] and selfish ambition exist, there will be disorder and every vile practice" (James 3:16).

Envy is unhappiness or discontent over the good fortune or success of others. We are envious when we are saddened at another's prosperity or when we rejoice in another's misfortune. This vice is not the same as the ordinary desire or wish we might have to be successful like someone else. Similarly, it is not the wish or desire to possess a certain talent.

"And whatever you do, in word or deed, do everything in the name of the Lord Jesus, giving thanks to God the Father through him."

(Colossians 3:17)

"And we desire each one of you to show the same earnestness in realizing the full assurance of hope until the end, so that you may not be sluggish, but imitators of those who through faith and patience inherit the promises" (Heb 6:11–12).

Sloth is excessive laziness or carelessness. It is unlike the other vices, because it is not an ordinary desire that is uncontrolled. It is really a lack of desire to do one's duties, particularly spiritual ones, because of the effort that is involved. It is not the same as a reasonable desire for times of rest or leisure.

We do not all have equal inclinations to these vices. Some of us must struggle more against temptations to envy, while others are more tempted by anger or gluttony. The first step on the path to holiness is to look at ourselves, try to recognize our weaknesses, and try to overcome them with God's help.

In the next chapter we will consider positive steps to holiness. We will study the virtues, what they are and how we can develop them.

Words to Know:
vocation   holiness   apostolate
habit   capital sins

100

". . . but as he who called you is holy, be holy yourselves in all your conduct: since it is written 'you shall be holy, for I am holy.' "

(1 Pet 1:15–16)

Q. 86 *What is vice?*
A vice is a bad habit that is acquired by repeating bad actions (CCC 1865).

Q. 87 *What are the principal vices?*
The principal vices are the seven capital sins of pride, avarice, lust, anger, gluttony, envy, and sloth (CCC 1866).

CHAPTER 15

The Life of Virtue

Make every effort to supplement your faith with virtue, and virtue with knowledge, and knowledge with self-control, and self-control with steadfastness, and steadfastness with godliness, and godliness with brotherly affection, and brotherly affection with love.

2 Peter 1:5–7

Just as there are habits that can be obstacles to our pursuit of holiness, there are also habits that can help us. If we consciously and willingly perform a good action frequently, we will be on the right path and acquire a disposition to do it again. Then it becomes more and more

part of us. It takes root in us. For example, if we tell the truth, or perform one generous act, we have not yet acquired the virtue of honesty or generosity. But if we repeat it we will be strengthened. The word *virtue* comes from the Latin word for strength.

A **virtue** is an abiding disposition of the soul, or power that enables a person to perform good actions easily and to avoid bad actions. It can be either *natural*—that is, acquired through repeated action, such as the virtue of honesty —or *supernatural*, that is, given to us by God.

The natural virtues in many ways resemble other habits. Take the example of a runner. At first running is difficult and a big effort for him. He endures and overcomes obstacles. Finally he can easily run for miles. He has the strength to do it. And then he even loves running.

So it is with virtues. We make the effort. We conquer the obstacles, and then we grow stronger, it becomes easier, and we finally love it. It is a joy for us. We conquer sin and grow closer to God. (Sinful habits give us a moment of pleasure, but unhappiness and a feeling of sadness in the end.) St. Benedict says that as we progress in virtue "our hearts shall be enlarged, and we shall run with unspeakable sweetness of love in the way of God's commandments."

And if one loves righteousness her labors are virtues; for she teaches self-control and prudence, justice and courage; nothing in life is more profitable for men than these (Wis 8:7).

The Cardinal Virtues

The natural, or *moral*, virtues enable us to act rightly in our conduct with other men. The chief moral virtues are the four **cardinal virtues**. They are called cardinal, from the Latin word for hinge, because they are the support or framework for all the other moral virtues. These four—prudence, justice, temperance (self-control), and fortitude (courage)—are the foundation for living a good life.

Prudence is the chief moral virtue, which directs all the others. Also called practical wisdom, this virtue enables us to determine what action is required in a given situation, and it moves us to do the action. The person who acts using good judgment at all times—knowing the right thing to do in every situation—has the virtue of prudence. Prudence requires that we know what to do and that we have the will to do it.

Prudence should be operating in all the decisions we make in our lives. We must learn to examine a situation clearly and to decide on the proper course of action with deliberation. For this to become a habit takes time and a great deal of experience.

Justice is the virtue that prompts us to give to others what is due to them—that is, what they deserve. Justice prompts us to pay debts owed to another, to keep promises that we have made, to obey laws made by those who have the authority, to keep secrets that someone entrusts to us, to play games fairly, and to respect the property of others. Justice directs us to act fairly and honestly toward others; it is commanded by the Seventh Commandment. For those in authority, acting justly sometimes means assigning punishments, since at times they may be deserved.

There are some debts that we can never fully repay—for example, the debts we owe to God who created us, to our parents for giving us life and raising us, or to our country. The respect, love, and loyalty that we show to them are derived from this virtue of justice.

Fortitude is the virtue that enables us to confront difficulties or dangers, perhaps even death, with courage and hope. With fortitude we are able to act calmly and reasonably even in the face of great dangers.

The martyrs of the Church all demonstrated the virtue of fortitude when they chose to remain faithful to Christ, despite the terrible deaths that awaited them. We might never be called upon to die for Christ, yet we need to develop the virtue of fortitude to be able to face the difficult moments in our lives—perhaps refusing to get drunk or use drugs when others encourage us to do this. St. Paul exhorts us to practice the virtue of fortitude when he says, in his letter to the Ephesians:

Take the whole armor of God, that you may be able to withstand in the evil day, and having done all, to stand (Eph 6:13).

Temperance is the virtue that enables us to control our passions and desires. This virtue allows us to act moderately and reasonably, so that we may use our bodies correctly. We often think of temperance as applying particularly to food and drink. This is true, but it also applies to all areas of our lives. The temperate person is one who eats the right amount, exercises the right amount, sleeps the right amount, and so on—that is, he is a person who habitually balances all activities of life.

Upon these four virtues hang many other moral virtues. One of these is the virtue of *religion*. Religion is the virtue by which we give to God the worship he deserves. This means that we praise him in a manner that is appropriate to his place as our Creator and Lord. This virtue stems from the cardinal virtue of justice.

Other Moral Virtues

Other moral virtues stemming from the cardinal virtues help us to counteract the seven capital sins. These good habits will replace the bad habits that can so easily develop.

Humility is the virtue opposed to pride. It leads one to have a just opinion of one's self and to give credit for our successes and gifts to God. Humility is related to the virtue of prudence, because it enables us to see the correct way to think about ourselves.

Liberality is the virtue opposed to covetousness. It enables a person to give freely of his money, possessions, talents, and so on to worthy purposes. Stemming from justice, liberality enables one to act fairly with his gifts and to serve the needs of others.

Chastity is the virtue opposed to lust. Chastity should not be seen *only* as self-control, moderation, and balance of sexual inclinations, but more importantly it should be understood in relation to the expression of human love. What does this mean? It means that sex is a great gift which by its nature entails complete donation of one person to another only in marriage. It therefore means abstaining from sex outside of marriage, so that the purest love can be given most completely to the spouse, or, in the case of priests and religious, to God in loving abstinence.

Meekness is the virtue opposed to anger. It is the virtue that enables us to be patient under injury or insult. The meek person is able to control his temper even in a trying or difficult situation. Because this takes a certain amount of spiritual strength or courage, meekness is related to the virtue of fortitude.

Moderation and *sobriety* are virtues opposed to gluttony. They enable one to use food and drink sensibly—enjoying them in the proper amounts and at suitable times. As forms of self-control, they stem from the cardinal virtue of temperance.

Brotherly love is the virtue opposed to envy. This virtue enables one to show true love for one's neighbor—praying for him, doing acts of kindness for him, and helping him in his needs. This virtue stems from the virtue of justice—for we are giving to another what is owed.

Diligence is the virtue opposed to sloth. This virtue enables us to do our work and carry out our religious duties—whatever they may be—with devotion and dedication. It stems from the virtue of prudence, for we see that hard work at our given tasks is the right way to act.

The Theological Virtues

The supernatural virtues are those that belong to us as Christians. Unlike the moral virtues, they cannot be acquired by repetition of certain actions, but are *infused*, given to us, by God. We receive them at Baptism, when we receive sanctifying grace. We exercise these virtues with the help of God, through the actual graces he gives us.

The supernatural virtues are faith, hope, and charity. Because these virtues come from God as well as direct us toward him, they are called *theological* virtues (theological in this sense means pertaining to God).

Faith is the virtue by which we believe all that God has revealed to us through Christ and his Church. The gift of faith is necessary, for it enables us to believe those mysteries—such as the Trinity—that are beyond the grasp of the human mind. We need faith in order to know our goal, which is heaven.

Hope is the virtue by which we trust in God's promises of eternal salvation. With hope we can find comfort in the words of Our Lord: "I am the resurrection and the life: he who believes in me, though he die, yet shall he live . . ." (Jn 11:25–26). Hope tells us that God, who promised us eternal salvation, will also give us the graces that we need to reach heaven.

Charity is the virtue by which we love God above all things for his own sake and love our neighbor as ourselves. The two Great Commandments of which Our Lord spoke to the scribe (Lk 10:25–28) can be summed up in the virtue of charity. This virtue enables us to love God above all, simply because he is good and deserves our love. We love our neighbors, including our enemies, because God loves them and because they, like ourselves, have been created in his image.

> So faith, hope, love abide, these three; but the greatest of these is love (1 Cor 13:13).

All three of these virtues are necessary if we are to reach heaven, but charity, which is love in its highest and fullest sense, is the greatest. It is the virtue that unites us most intimately with God and our neighbor. It is through charity that we are moved to obey God's law and to perform good actions. Every virtue we have studied so far becomes radiant, beautiful, and new when infused by this love. As St. Paul says, all things are made new through Jesus Christ (see 2 Cor 5:17).

While the theological virtues cannot be acquired through repetition of certain acts, we can strengthen them by our actions. Through prayer we open ourselves to God's grace so that we can receive these great gifts. If we *really* want them and *really* strive after them, then we

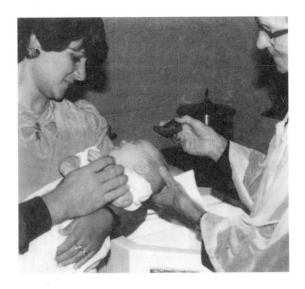

will receive them. Christ says, "Ask, and it shall be given you; . . . knock, and it will be opened to you" (Mt 7:7). Just as our bodies require exercise to remain in shape, so these virtues must be exercised if they are to help us reach heaven. In general, we can develop and exercise these virtues by making acts of faith, hope, and charity.

Faith is strengthened when we profess and defend our faith, and when we study and think about the meaning of the mysteries of the faith. It is also made stronger by the good actions that we do, since ". . . faith apart from works is dead" (James 2:26). We can exercise hope by accepting the will of God, trusting him to care for us as he cares for the birds of the air and the lilies of the field (Lk 12:22–34). By doing so we can avoid becoming unduly anxious or upset by life—even by trials or sorrows. We strengthen the virtue of charity by observing the Commandments, as Our Lord instructed us: "He who has my commandments and keeps them, he it is who loves me. . . . If a man loves me, he will keep my word" (Jn 14:21, 23). We also exercise charity by doing the works of mercy, which we will consider in the next chapter.

Living the virtuous life—practicing these virtues daily—is not easy. It is, in fact, a great challenge. But it is a challenge that we can meet, because we have God's help through prayer and the sacraments. In our struggle we should remember the saints. They are the proof for us that the life of virtue is possible. They also show that virtue will be rewarded by God.

Finally, we should recall the example of Our Lord himself. Christ is both God and man. But he showed us as man the perfect way to live as a human being.

Words to Know:
    virtue   cardinal virtues

Q. 88   *What is a virtue?*
A virtue is an abiding habit of the soul to do good (CCC 1803).

Q. 89   *What are the two kinds of virtues?*
The two kinds of virtues are natural and supernatural virtues. Natural virtues are acquired by repeating good acts. The supernatural virtues (also known as the theological virtues) cannot be acquired or even exercised by our own power. They come to us as gifts from God (CCC 1804, 1812).

Q. 90   *What is a moral virtue?*
A moral virtue (also called a human virtue) is a habit of doing good, acquired by repeatedly doing good acts (CCC 1804).

Q. 91   *What are the principal moral virtues?*
The principal moral virtues are religion, by which we give God the worship owed to him, and the four cardinal virtues: prudence, justice, fortitude, and temperance (CCC 1805).

Q. 92   *Why are certain virtues called cardinal virtues?*
Certain virtues are called cardinal virtues because they are pivotal and the support, or framework, for all the other moral virtues (CCC 1805).

Q. 93   *What is the virtue of prudence?*
Prudence is the virtue that directs our actions to the true good in every situation and enables us to choose the right means of achieving it (CCC 1806).

Q. 94   *What is the virtue of justice?*
Justice is the virtue by which we always give to God or our neighbor what is due him (CCC 1807).

Q. 95   *What is the virtue of fortitude?*
Fortitude is the virtue by which we confront with courage any difficulty or danger, even death itself, for the service of God and the welfare of neighbor (CCC 1808).

Q. 96   *What is the virtue of temperance?*
Temperance is the virtue by which we hold our passions and desires, especially the sensual ones, under control (CCC 1809).

Q. 97   *What are the theological virtues?*
The theological virtues are faith, hope, and charity (CCC 1813).

Q. 98   *Why are certain virtues called theological virtues?*
Certain virtues are called theological virtues because they have God himself for their origin, motive, and object (CCC 1812–13).

Q. 99 *How do we receive and exercise the theological virtues?*

We receive the theological virtues together with sanctifying grace by means of the sacraments. We exercise them with the hope of actual graces, namely the good thoughts and inspirations with which God moves and helps us in every good act that we do (CCC 2025).

Q. 100 *Which is the most excellent among the theological virtues?*

The most excellent among the theological virtues is charity, which unites us intimately to God and to our neighbor (CCC 1826).

Q. 101 *What is faith?*

Faith is the theological virtue by which we believe what God has revealed as it is taught by the Church (CCC 1814).

Q. 102 *What is hope?*

Hope is the theological virtue by which we trust in God for the graces necessary to obey him and merit eternal life (CCC 1817).

Q. 103 *What is charity?*

Charity is the theological virtue by which we love God above all things for his own sake, and love our neighbor as ourselves because we love God (CCC 1822).

Q. 104 *Why must we love God for his own sake?*

We must love God for his own sake because he is supremely good and the source of every good thing (CCC 2055).

Q. 105 *Why must we love our neighbor?*

We must love our neighbor because God has commanded that we love one another and because every human being has been created in God's image (CCC 1823).

Q. 106 *Why are we obliged to love our enemies?*

We are obliged to love our enemies because they are also our neighbors and Jesus Christ explicitly commanded us to love our enemies (CCC 1825, 2303).

Q. 107 *How do we give proof of our faith?*

We give proof of our faith by professing it, defending it, and living according to its teachings (CCC 1816, 2471).

Q. 108 *How do we give proof of our hope?*

We give proof of our hope by living in peaceful acceptance of the promises of Christ (CCC 1817–18).

Q. 109 *How do we prove our charity?*

We prove our charity by observing the commandments of God, living in love, and giving of ourselves for the sake of the Kingdom according to our vocation (CCC 1827–28).

CHAPTER 16

The Works of Mercy and Happiness

"Blessed are the merciful, for they shall obtain mercy."

Matthew 5:7

We grow in virtue, particularly in practicing the *works of mercy*. In these acts we show our love for Christ by helping our neighbor. Our Lord told us, "Then the just will ask him: 'Lord, when did we see you hungry and feed you or see you thirsty and give you drink? When did we welcome you away from home or clothe you in your nakedness? When did we visit you when you were ill or in prison?' The King will answer them: 'I assure you, as often as you did it for one of my least brothers, you did it for me' " (Mt 25:37–40).

Since we have both bodies and souls—and both require care—the works of mercy are divided into two groups. We care for our neighbors' souls and spiritual needs through the spiritual works of mercy. We care for their bodies and physical needs through corporal works of mercy (the Latin word *corpus* means "body").

Because our souls are the most important part of our human nature—the part by which we can think, know, and freely choose good or evil—the seven spiritual works of mercy are the most important. As we consider each of

them, think of how you can practice these in your life. Remember that the heart and soul of each of these works is love; love is their moving force.

Spiritual Works

Admonish the sinner. Because sin separates one from God, it is truly an act of love to help another person realize the seriousness of sin and the need for forgiveness. This does not mean humiliating someone in public or acting as if we ourselves have never sinned. Rather, we should quietly and tactfully steer our friends away from occasions of sin or encourage those who have sinned to seek forgiveness in the sacrament of Penance, giving them hope that they will be able to overcome sinful ways with the mercy of God.

Instruct the ignorant. Helping a person to learn or understand the truths that God has revealed to us is a second way to nourish another's spiritual life. Our religion teachers and parents, of course, do this for us, but there are also other ways to practice this work of mercy

as well. There are many people who have not heard the message of the gospel in its fullness. We can often find opportunities to tell them about it, remembering the words of Our Lord:

> No one after lighting a lamp puts it in a cellar or under a bushel, but on a stand, that those who enter may see the light (Lk 11:33).

We have been given the "light of faith" and should not hide it but should let it shine forth. However, we must avoid preaching or acting as if we know all the answers.

Counsel the doubtful. To counsel someone means giving him advice or guidance. Those who most need this counsel are people who are weak in the virtues of faith and hope. For example, someone may reject certain beliefs of the faith—or at least question them—or may fall into despair, doubting that God will forgive him for his sins. These people need loving guidance and encouragement to strengthen them, thus bringing them closer to God once more.

Comfort the sorrowful. Suffering is a part of our life in this world. Indeed, Our Lord told us that those who wish to follow him must first take up their cross, just as he took up his Cross for us. Each of us has our own specific crosses that Our Lord asks us to bear out of love for him. This is not always easy, and this work of mercy reminds us that we should help one another to bear the sufferings in our lives. Sometimes a word of love and understanding can help. Sometimes a kind deed can lighten the burden of someone else's suffering.

111

Bear wrongs patiently. It is important to remember that it is better to suffer an injustice than to be guilty of committing one ourselves. In his Sermon on the Mount, Our Lord said:

> I say to you. . . . Love your enemies, do good to those who hate you, bless those who curse you, pray for those who abuse you. To him who strikes you on the cheek, offer the other also; and from him who takes away your cloak do not withhold your coat as well (Lk 6:27–29).

This true charity is the mark of the Christian, and we must learn to be patient and strong when we are the victims of injustice. It is by such actions that we may draw others to Christ.

Forgive all injuries. Not only must we patiently bear these wrongs, we must also forgive those who injure us. In the *Lord's Prayer*, which Jesus taught us, we say, "Forgive us our trespasses, as we forgive those who trespass against us" (Mt 6:12). This means the measure by which we forgive will be the measure by which God will forgive us. By forgiving others we imitate the love that Christ shows for us. He offers forgiveness to all—even those who put him to death on the Cross.

Pray for the living and the dead. We have already seen that the Communion of Saints means that we can pray for one another. This act of love is one of the easiest—and one of the most important—ways to help others. We recall that charity toward our neighbor includes our enemies, and our prayers should extend to them as well. When we pray for those who have died, let us remember not only our relatives and friends, but also those souls who are most forgotten.

Corporal Works

The seven corporal works of mercy are those acts of love that Our Lord spoke about when he described the Last Judgment. To those who practice these works Our Lord will say:

> Come, O blessed of my Father, inherit the kingdom prepared for you from the foundation of the world; for I was hungry and you gave me food; I was thirsty and you gave me drink; I was a stranger and you welcomed me; I was naked and you clothed me; I was sick and you visited me; I was in prison and you came to me (Mt 25:34–36).

Feed the hungry, give drink to the thirsty, and clothe the naked. Most of us have been greatly blessed by God. Nevertheless, there are many people in the world—even some in our country—who lack many of the basic needs of life. We must not neglect these people. It is an obligation of charity to help them. While we may not be able to help these people directly or dramatically, we can contribute money or possessions to groups whose works are such charitable activities. For example, there may be an organization in your parish—such as the St. Vincent de Paul Society—which carries out these works of mercy.

These works of mercy start in the family. Parents are responsible for seeing that their children are fed and clothed. In the same way, when the children are older they are responsible for taking care of these needs for their aging parents. At this point in our lives we can practice these works of mercy in simple ways. For example, we can prepare lunch for a hungry brother or sister or share some of our clothes with others in our family. Families together can reach out to other poorer families. These acts of mercy will prepare us for greater works as we grow older.

Visit the imprisoned. There are many kinds of people in prison. There is the hardened criminal. Some great conversions have taken place among the most hardened, and perhaps

The Spiritual Works of Mercy	The Corporal Works of Mercy
Admonish the sinner	Feed the hungry
Instruct the ignorant	Give drink to the thirsty
Counsel the doubtful	Clothe the naked
Comfort the sorrowful	Visit the imprisoned
Bear wrongs patiently	Shelter the homeless
Forgive all injuries	Visit the sick
Pray for the living and the dead	Bury the dead

the grace they received came through the prayers or kindness of people who knew them. There are some who were weak and made mistakes but are now sorry for what they have done. These people need to be encouraged, so that they will continue to reform their lives. Some are innocent. If we are able, we should help them obtain justice. In the meantime, they need our support.

There are still other people who are not in jail, but whose state in life can be like a prison —separating them from other people and the support such contact brings. For example, some who, for a long period of time, must care for a sick relative at home may need our visits to help him accept his present cross.

Shelter the homeless. There are many homeless people in our cities. We should pay attention to their great need. For example, Trevor Ferrell, a twelve-year-old boy in Philadelphia brought the street people blankets from his own home. The word got around and soon the whole neighborhood was helping. Finally they even rented a house for the homeless. We may not always be able to do much directly for those people who are homeless. However, we can practice this work of mercy by being willing to share our homes with someone in need —for example, a friend whose home has been damaged by a fire or flood. We can also willingly share our own room with a brother or sister if this is needed in our family.

Visit the sick. The sick are often frightened and may be in particular need of encouragement. It is not always easy for us who are healthy to understand the suffering sick people go through. Visiting them may give them the strength they need to bear their cross. Perhaps they may need us in some practical way. Christ can touch them through our acts of love.

Bury the dead. The final act of mercy is mentioned in the Old Testament. The angel Raphael praised Tobias for this charitable act:

And when you buried the dead, I was likewise present with you. When you did not hesitate to rise and leave your dinner in order to go and lay out the dead, your good deed was not hidden from me (Tob 12:12–13).

By this action we show respect for the body, because it is part of the human being. We can practice this work of mercy by attending a funeral of someone we knew—and offering consolation to those who are bereaved—or by respecting cemeteries, perhaps leaving flowers at the grave site of a relative.

By living the virtuous life and practicing the works of mercy, we will be *happy* for ever with God in heaven. This is the happiness of which Our Lord spoke in the Sermon on the Mount (Mt 5:3–11). He promised this happiness to those who live the Christian life, which he summarized in the eight *Beatitudes*.

"Beatify" means "to make happy." A beatitude is a special happiness or blessing of a spiritual nature. These eight Beatitudes are the promises for happiness that Christ makes to those who faithfully accept his teaching and follow his example.

The happiness of which Our Lord speaks, however, is not what the world identifies with happiness—money, power, fame, and so on. Even when such things bring us pleasure or happiness, it is fleeting. The happiness that belongs to the *meek, the pure in heart*, and so on is the lasting happiness of eternal life. This happiness brings us true joy and peace even in our life on earth. It is the happiness which no one can take from us. It lasts for ever.

Q. 110 *What are the spiritual works of mercy?*
The spiritual works of mercy are admonish the sinner; instruct the ignorant; counsel the doubtful; comfort the sorrowful; bear wrongs patiently; forgive all injuries; pray for the living and the dead (CCC 2447).

Q. 111 *What are the corporal works of mercy?*
The corporal works of mercy are feed the hungry; give drink to the thirsty; clothe the naked; visit the imprisoned; shelter the homeless; visit the sick; bury the dead (CCC 2447).

CHAPTER 17

Vocations: The Religious Life and the Priesthood

Greater love has no man than this, that a man lay down his life for his friends.

John 15:1

"Under the impulse of love, which the Holy Spirit pours into their hearts, they live more and more for Christ and for his Body, the Church. The more fervently, therefore, they join themselves to Christ by this gift of their whole life, the fuller does the Church's life become and the more vigorous and fruitful its apostolate" *(PC, 1).*

In an earlier chapter we spoke of the vocation that all of us share as Christians—to follow Christ and ultimately to be with God in heaven. Yet, each must pursue this goal differently, according to his own temperament and particular call from God. The vocation of most Christians is the life of a layman or laywoman in the world. For others, though, it will be the priestly or religious life.

We have seen that, from the beginning of Christianity, some in the Church have directly consecrated their lives to God by a vow. Although not everyone is called to this life, Our Lord invites many to follow him in this way. In the Gospels he tells us of the reward that will be given to those who answer this call:

And every one who has left houses or brothers or sisters or father or mother or children or lands for my name's sake, will receive a hundredfold, and inherit eternal life (Mt 19:29).

The call to the priesthood or the religious life is a vocation to follow Christ most perfectly on earth. Once Our Lord was approached by a rich young man who asked what he must do to have eternal life. Our Lord told him:

"If you would enter life, keep the commandments. . . ." The young man said to him, "All these I have observed; what do I still lack?" Jesus said to him, "If you would be perfect, go, sell what you possess and give to the poor, and you will have treasure in heaven; and come, follow me" (Mt 19:17, 20–21).

Here Jesus was speaking of the call to the religious life—following the counsels of perfection.

Although this vocation is the highest call, God does not intend everyone to live the religious life. Each of us must seek holiness in the state that God wants us to live. The consecrat-

115

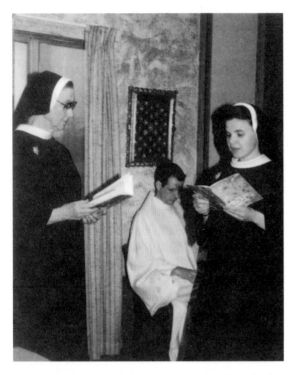

ed life calls for great generosity. Objectively, religious life is the most perfect. This does not mean that a lay person cannot attain perfection. Every vocation leads to holiness. Everyone must try to find out what God calls him to.

Religious Life

The religious life consists in following the three **evangelical counsels**, also known as the counsels of perfection. These are recommendations for perfect love taught and practiced by Christ—poverty, chastity, and obedience. Those who follow these counsels take *vows* (free, deliberate promises made to God) to keep each one. They willingly give up certain good things of this life—money and possessions, marriage, and liberty—in order to devote themselves more completely to loving and serving God and neighbor. These vows set a person free from temporal goods, so that he may freely give himself to love of God and neighbor.

The first counsel is poverty. The person who takes this vow gives up his earthly possessions in order to follow Christ. In our modern world, where so much emphasis is placed upon jobs, money, and possessions, this is indeed a sacrifice, even for one who is not rich.

Through religious life Christ calls for a life of total consecration in individual service to God and to one's neighbor. This means that you give to God the highest natural goods. One of these is the loving union with another person in marriage and family life. Human love in marriage is a holy thing, which Our Lord has blessed. Thus the sacrifice involved in giving this up is truly great. By the vow of chastity a person consecrates himself more completely to God, surrendering the good of marriage.

Since one might fulfill the counsels of poverty and chastity but still be filled with love of self, God asks one final sacrifice of the person who dedicates his life to him. He asks that one surrender his own personal preferences and wishes. This is the vow of obedience. The person who follows this path then gives up his liberty, submitting himself completely through his legitimate religious superiors, to the will of God as it is manifest in the Church.

One who enters the religious life, practicing the vows of poverty, chastity, and obedience, does so in imitation of Christ himself. At his death Our Lord had nothing; the soldiers even cast lots for the clothes he had been wearing (Mt 27:35). At one time he said of himself, ". . . . the Son of man has nowhere to lay his head" (Mt 8:20). We know Our Lord never married; he spent his public life preaching and teaching the Good News. Most important, he submitted his will to his Father in heaven. This was particularly demonstrated on the eve of his death, when he prayed in the Garden of Gethsemane. Knowing what lay ahead of him, he said:

Father, if thou art willing, remove this cup from me; nevertheless not my will, but thine, be done (Lk 22:42).

Those in the religious life are an example to all people. They remind us of the importance of placing God first in our lives. Although we are not all called to sacrifice these goods, even those living in the world are called to place their love of God above the love of possessions, family, and self.

As we have seen, various religious communities have been officially instituted throughout history for those who are called to the religious life. There are communities for men and others for women. In both, members live a community life according to a particular rule. Prayer and contemplation ordered to a more perfect love of God and neighbor are the basic work of all religious communities. For some communities this is their principal work. These members of *contemplative* orders spend their days in prayer, by which they serve God and the entire Church. This is a great work that helps the world tremendously, since there are so many who forget God. The **contemplatives** usually live a *cloistered* life, separated completely from the world and working within their monasteries or convents to support themselves. The Benedictine and Cistercian communities, as well as some Carmelite communities, are examples of the contemplative religious life.

Other religious communities dedicate themselves to a more active service of God and neighbor by engaging in various works of mercy —both corporal and spiritual. These active orders may operate schools, hospitals, or

"If you would be perfect, go, and sell what you possess and give to the poor, and you will have treasure in heaven; then come, follow me."

(Matthew 19:21)

orphanages. There is one community of sisters who both visit and pray for those in prison, helping them to reform their lives. This order has, in fact, many sisters who were once prisoners themselves. Mother Teresa's Missionaries of Charity are an active community who care for those who are dying and perform other active works. This active work, however, must always flow from and be an expression of the prayer life of these religious communities. Prayer, then, even in the active religious life is the basis for all their work.

Priesthood

There is a very special calling of Christ which is of great importance in the Church. It is not something one can simply choose, but something one is called to. It is the priesthood, the sacrament of Holy Orders. This call to exercise the priestly power of Christ and to be "another Christ" is a great honor but also a great and beautiful sacrifice. Those who have received Holy Orders share most perfectly in the redeeming work of Jesus Christ. They are the ministers of grace to the Church, as they administer the sacraments.

Some priests or clergy are members of a religious community. The **clergy** is made up of deacons, priests, and bishops. Most ordained ministers in the Church have been called to serve Christ as *diocesan clergy*. They are members of a particular diocese, often serving in parish work.

At their ordination the diocesan clergy promise obedience to their bishop, and bishops owe their obedience to the Pope. In the Latin rite the priests do not marry, taking a vow (or promise) of **celibacy**. However, in the Latin rite permanent deacons may be married, and in some Eastern rites priests may be married. Those who are married do promise, however, not to marry again if their spouse dies. Diocesan clergy are not bound to take a vow of

---

Church Teaching

"This then is the primary purpose, this the central idea of Christian virginity: to aim only at the divine, to turn thereto the whole mind and soul; to want to please God in everything, to think of him continually, to consecrate body and soul to him."

(Holy Virginity, Pius XII, March 25, 1954)

118

poverty. They may own things and usually receive a small salary for their personal expenses. They try to live a simple life in order to imitate Our Lord more closely and to be a witness for Christ to the world.

The Church needs many men and women to follow Christ, answering God's call to the religious life and the priesthood. We should pray to know if this is God's will for us. Even if this is not our vocation, we should pray that those who are called will joyfully respond, for:

The harvest is plentiful, but the laborers are few; pray therefore the Lord of the harvest to send out laborers into his harvest (Mt 9:37–38).

Words to Know:
evangelical counsels
clergy   contemplative   celibacy

"Father, you call all who believe in you to grow perfect in love by following in the footsteps of Christ your Son. May those whom you have chosen to serve you as religious provide by their way of life a convincing sign of your Kingdom for the Church and the whole world. We ask this through Our Lord Jesus Christ, your Son, who lives and reigns with you and the Holy Spirit, one God, for ever and ever. Amen."

(Sacramentary, Mass for Religious Vocations)

Q. 112 *Is the priesthood a great dignity?*

Yes, the priesthood is a great dignity because of its powers to consecrate the Eucharist and to forgive sins. Those who receive this great dignity have the sublime mission of leading men to holiness and the life of the blessed (CCC 1563).

Q. 113 *How may one enter into Holy Orders?*

To enter Holy Orders, one must be called by God and submit his desire to the authority of the Church. He must have the vocation to Holy Orders, with the disposition required by the sacred ministry (CCC 1578).

Q. 114 *What are the evangelical counsels?*

The evangelical counsels are vows of poverty, chastity, and obedience, and are called evangelical because they were given to us by Jesus in the Gospels (CCC 915, 944).

Q. 115 *What is religious life?*

Religious life is a gift of self to God through public profession of the evangelical counsels. The religious life gives witness to Christ's union with the Church (CCC 925).

CHAPTER 18

The Lay Apostolate

"Go into all the world and preach the gospel to the whole creation."
Mark 16:15

"From the fact of their union with Christ the head flows the laymen's right and duty to be apostles. Inserted as they are in the Mystical Body of Christ by baptism and strengthened by the power of the Holy Spirit in confirmation, it is by the Lord himself that they are assigned to the apostolate." (AA, 3).

While God calls some to serve him in the religious life or the priesthood, he calls most people to serve him in the world. Those members of the Church who are not ordained or do not belong to a religious community are called the **laity**.

The laity share the universal call to holiness with those in religious life. They, like priests, sisters, and brothers, must develop a strong spiritual life, uniting themselves with Christ through prayer, work, and the sacraments. This form of the spiritual life, however, will be different for each group because of their activities and obligations.

In addition to this universal call to holiness, members of the laity are also called to serve the Church in various capacities. This service begins within their individual parish communities. They may also serve the Church at the diocesan, national, or even international levels.

Finally, the laity, like the religious, are called to be witnesses of Christ and his Church. Both by their word and their example, laymen are called to bring Christ's gospel message to the world. Because their manner of life is the same as that of others in the world—raising families, working, and so on—they may at times be more effective witnesses of the gospel than are those in religious life.

Unlike priests and religious, who are called to live *separated from* the world, the laity must live *in* the world. They must "permeate society with the leaven of the gospel." The laity must be the "salt of the earth" (Mt 5:13), drawing the world to Christ. This means that they must try to bring Christian justice and charity into all the activities of human life—social, economic, industrial, political, cultural, and recreational activities.

All of these are temporal (worldly) goods, and it is the specific vocation of the layman to sanctify them. The grace of Christ does not take the place of nature but respects the natural order and perfects it.

The layman is especially called to use the three great goods that religious freely give up —wealth, sexuality, and independence. The laity are called to use their money and possessions for the good of the Church, of their families and of those in need. Most are also called to marry and raise a family, thus bringing new souls to Christ. Finally, they are called to use their freedom to make Christ present everywhere in the world.

Even though the layman's vocation is to live in the world, he must always keep in mind the warning of Our Lord that we live in the world but not be of the world. The laity must work to renew the temporal order, drawing all toward God. But at the same time, they must strive to keep themselves free from the corruptions of the world. St. Paul wrote, "Do not be conformed to this world" (Rom 12:2).

The lay apostolate encompasses both work and *leisure* (those activities that are not work and are done for their own sake). The layman must sanctify himself as well as the world through these activities.

Each person is called to sanctify his ordinary labor, using it as a means of serving God. For you, as students, your principal "work" or duty right now is to study, learning basic skills and preparing yourself for future studies and work. You must, then, use your studies and

"Help me spread your fragrance everywhere. Flood my soul with your spirit and life. Penetrate and possess my whole being so utterly that all my life may be a witness, a radiance of yours. Shine through me and be so in me that every soul I come in contact with may be aware of your presence in me. Let them look up and see no longer me, but only you, Lord Jesus."

(Cardinal Newman)

Church Teaching

"Laymen ought to take on themselves as their distinctive task this renewal of the temporal order. Guided by the light of the gospel and the mind of the Church, prompted by Christian love, they should act in this domain in a different way and in their own specific manner. As citizens among citizens they must bring to their cooperation with others their own special competence and act on their own responsibility; everywhere and always they have to seek the justice of the Kingdom of God" (AA, 7).

homework to praise God. This means beginning now to do the best you can in your schoolwork, so that it may be a fitting offering to God. The same is true of any duties you may have at home —for example, doing the dishes, caring for the yard—or at a job. The layman is also called to sanctify his leisure—serving God through excellence in art, music, athletics, and the like.

The lay vocation embraces both the married and the unmarried life. Both are called to live chastity in different ways, according to their state. While most of the laity are called to the married state, there are some people who live the lay life as unmarried persons. These people continue to live in the world and have no intention of entering a religious community. While this calling may not be for many, those who are called to the single life in the world are given the graces they need to become holy through the sacrament of Confirmation. They also gain strength from the sacraments of Penance and the Eucharist.

The single state may be chosen by some people who desire to serve others in the world more fully than they could if they had a family. For example, it was common in our country in the nineteenth century for women teachers to remain unmarried, so that they could devote themselves more fully to educating others. Others may remain unmarried because obligations in justice or charity require it. For example, one might remain single in order to be able to care for aged parents or other relatives who need one's care.

Most lay people however, live the married life. This state is a great vocation, instituted and blessed by God at the Creation of the world. We will consider the married state in the next chapter.

Words to Know:
laity

Q. 116 *Who are the laity?*
The laity are all the faithful people who have been baptized, and therefore are members of the Church, but are not clergy or members of a religious community. The laity participate in the priestly, prophetic, and kingly ministry of Christ in the world (CCC 897).

CHAPTER 19

Marriage and the Family

"... What therefore God has joined together, let no man put asunder."

Matthew 19:6

"God created man in his own image and likeness: calling him to existence through love*, he called him at the same time* for love*" (FC, 11).*

There are two main vocations to love: marriage and virginity or celibacy. The vocation to marriage is a vocation to a specific kind of human love (conjugal love), blessed by God and instituted by him at the creation of the world. In the first two chapters of Genesis we read about the creation of the world and the institution of married life.

In the above quote, the Pope refers to the words of Genesis 1:27 telling us that God made man and woman in his own image. This means that they are different from everything else in the world that God had created until then. They have an intellect and free will as God has. They are persons, a man and a woman, equal in dignity—"male and female he created them." God is love, and since they were made in his image they were made to love God and each other. The words of Genesis continue, "God blessed them." Thus they formed the first community of love, an image of the Trinity, which is the divine community of love.

Then God said to them, "Be fruitful and multiply, and fill the earth . . ." (Gen 1:28).

This tells us that God meant this community of love, which is marriage, to bear fruit. He gave them a share in his act of creation. The fruit of marriage is children. This is its first purpose. God intended that through the loving union of man and woman in marriage, children be brought forth. They are its crowning glory.

In the second chapter of Genesis we read more about the vocation of marriage:

The Lord God said, "It is not good that the man should be alone; I will make him a helper fit for him" . . . and the rib which the Lord God had taken from the man he made into a woman and brought her to the man. Then the man said, "This at last is bone of my bones and flesh of my flesh. . . ." Therefore a man leaves his father and mother and cleaves to his wife, and they become one flesh (Gen 2:18, 22–24).

Here God reveals to us that marriage, which by its nature is a union of love, has as a second purpose *mutual love* and *support* of the husband and wife. The man and woman united in marriage are to support one another in life. They are to help one another in their tasks on earth—primarily raising their children. Through marriage they become *one* and are no longer simply individuals. They are called to sacrifice some of their individual freedom for the sake of a greater good—the new family they have formed.

We also learn from the above quote that the man and woman shall become one flesh—that is, the union in marriage is one of body as well as of soul. There is a total giving, under God, of the whole person to the other. There can be no total conjugal self-giving apart from marriage. Total self-giving means giving of oneself, until death, exclusively to one person. You enter freely and consciously into marriage. You make a public promise in front of witnesses which, once made, you are no longer free to take back. You even give up the right to decide otherwise in the future. Total giving of self also means accepting all the consequences, which includes openness to the gift of life.

Since bodily union is an expression of the total self-giving of two persons, it is a lie if it takes place between two unmarried persons. If your body expresses, "I am yours for ever," but your mind knows that is not true, then you are lying. That is why sex outside of marriage is a lie. It is also, of course, fornication or adultery.

The Sacrament of Marriage

The married state has been blessed by Our Lord as well. At the beginning of his public life, Our Lord attended a wedding feast where he worked his first miracle (Jn 2:1–11). By his presence at this wedding, Christ blessed the vocation of marriage. He also raised marriage above the natural level to the dignity of a sacrament. Thus, the baptized man and woman who unite themselves in marriage receive from Christ the graces that they need to live this life. These are special graces to help them overcome obstacles, bear their crosses, and become better spouses and parents.

For the Christian the natural ends, or pur-

poses, of marriage are raised to a supernatural level. The bearing and raising of children are not simply for life here on earth. Christian parents raise children that they may eventually be united for ever with God in heaven. Similarly, the Christian husband and wife not only support one another in mutual love but, even more importantly, must help one another to know, love, and serve God so that they may reach heaven. This is called the *mutual sanctification* of the spouses.

Christ also emphasized the *indissoluble* nature of marriage. He taught us that the union of husband and wife is a lifelong union, which ends only with death. On one occasion, when Our Lord was questioned by the Pharisees about divorce, he quoted the passage from the second chapter of Genesis and then said:

What therefore God has joined together, let no man put asunder. . . . I say to you: whoever divorces his wife . . . and marries another, commits adultery; and he who marries a divorced woman, commits adultery (Mt 19:6, 9).

Thus did Our Lord make clear that marriage must be a permanent state on earth. He himself taught this on his authority as Son of God, for even in the Gospels we see that his contemporaries accepted divorce. Because the indissolubility of marriage is often rejected in today's world as well, the Christian must be an example and witness to the world.

The New Testament also teaches us about the supernatural element of marriage. In his letter to the Christian community in Ephesus, St. Paul reminds us of the mutual obligation of husbands and wives to love one another: "Husbands, love your wives, as Christ loved the church . . . and let the wife see that she respects her husband" (Eph 5:25, 33). Thus, we are to love one another with Christ himself as our model.

The Family

As we have seen, husband and wife unite in marriage to form a new community—the family. The family is the basic unit of society. It is in the family that new human beings are brought into the world. It is here that we first learn how to live in society. And it is in the family that children are first taught and prepared for their place in the Church and in society. There are then obligations for both parents and children in the family.

In addition to helping one another to serve God and neighbor and thus reach heaven, the state of marriage places other obligations and responsibilities on the husband and wife in their roles as parents.

1. The first obligation is that they must be open to the gift of life. This means that they must accept children as coming from God and destined for God. While it is true that not all marriages will be blessed with children, this openness to children must always be present. In childless marriages the couples can glorify God through their union of love and their mutual sanctification. They are called to be spiritually fruitful through works of mercy such as, for instance, adoption or foster care of children.

2. The second obligation of parents is to care for those children whom God has given them. The basic needs of life must be met first. Satisfying physical needs, however, is not sufficient for preparing children for the world or for eternal life.

3. The third obligation of parents is to educate and form their children so that they will be able to lead good and useful lives on earth and, finally, to attain salvation in heaven. Naturally, parents must see to the basic instruction of their children—reading, mathematics, and the like. More importantly, parents are responsible for their moral and religious education. They must care for the spiritual needs of their children—not simply their physical needs. One of the first duties of Christian parents, for example, is to have their children baptized.

Since moral, religious, and intellectual education begin very early in life, parents are the first teachers of their children, by both word and example. They are also the *primary* educators of their children. This means that the obligation for educating their children belongs first to the parents. Even though most parents eventually delegate their role of educator to the school, they should not abandon their role as the primary educators. Parents must continue to teach their children and help to form their moral characters.

Filial Piety

Children also have obligations and duties within the family, and must develop the virtue known as **filial piety**. This is the virtue of giving honor and respect to our parents, who are immediately responsible for our existence and well-being. Like the virtue of religion, filial piety is a part of justice and is an acknowledgement of the debt that we owe to our parents.

Filial piety requires us to obey our parents since they have been given authority from God to raise us. In this we can model ourselves on Jesus, who was obedient to Mary and Joseph. "And he went down with them and came to Nazareth, and was obedient to them" (Lk 2:51). This obligation is proper to us until we reach adulthood and are responsible for our own lives.

Filial piety, however, does not end with our maturity. We are still obliged to honor and respect our parents. We must recognize the great work they have undertaken with God and should show them esteem and gratitude. That is what the Fourth Commandment is all about.

Finally, filial piety requires us to care for our parents in their old age or infirmity. The Word of God in the book of Sirach reminds us of this duty: "O son, help your father in his old age, and do not grieve him as long as he lives" (Sir 3:12).

Behold, how good and pleasant it is when brothers dwell in unity! (Ps 133:1).

Children also have the duty within the family to love and respect their brothers and sisters. This charity should be offered to everyone, but since we share a more intimate bond with the members of our family, it is even more important there. Often this is difficult to achieve, but we must each work to make our homes centers of Christian charity and unity.

Finally, children also have an obligation to respect the authority belonging to those who teach them. Since parents may delegate some of their authority to the school, just as they respect, honor, and obey their parents, children must respect, honor, and obey those who teach them. We recognize this special role of the school as taking the place of our parents temporarily when we call the school our *alma mater*, which means "loving or nourishing mother." Truly we are nourished by the school as we are nourished by our parents.

In addition to this, as children grow older, they must take upon themselves more and more responsibility for their education. This is particularly important in our religious education. Often people study their faith during their youth, are confirmed, and then do not pay any further attention to their religious development. Our knowledge of our faith does not end with our Confirmation. Rather, we must, as adults in the Church, take charge of our religious development and continue to grow in the knowledge and love of God.

The married state, through family life, prepares us for our place in society. In the next chapter we will examine the role of the Christian in the state and the world.

Words to Know:
filial piety

Q. 117 *What happens in the Sacrament of Matrimony?*

In the Sacrament of Matrimony, a man and a woman are united indissolubly as Jesus Christ and his Spouse, the Church, are united. Through the sacrament they are given special graces to live in a holy way and to raise and educate their children in a Christian manner (CCC 1601).

Q. 118 *What duties do the spouses assume?*

The spouses assume the duties of living together in a holy way helping each other with unfailing affection in their temporal and spiritual necessities, and raising their children in the Catholic faith (CCC 1641).

"God created man in his own image and likeness: calling him to existence through love, he called him at the same time for love."

(FC, 11)

CHAPTER 20

The Christian in the World

By me kings reign, and rulers decree what is just; by me princes rule, and nobles govern the earth.

Proverbs 8:15–16

Just as men and women naturally come together to form families, human beings also join together to form larger societies. Not only are we members of a family, but we are citizens of a city or town, state, and a nation. Just as our parents have legitimate authority over us in the family, so do the officials of the civil government. St. Paul reminds us that their authority, like that of our parents, comes from God:

> Let every person be subject to the governing authorities. For there is no authority except from God. . . . Therefore he who resists the authorities resists what God has appointed. . . (Rom 13:1–2).

Human nature, as God created it, calls human beings to form civil societies. Civil society belongs to an order established by God. The purpose of civil society is to promote and ensure the **common good** of its members. The common good is the welfare of the whole community, not just an individual. The common good includes everything in society that helps people, either as groups or individuals, to reach more easily their fulfillment as human beings. In order to promote the common good of the whole community the state has the authority to make just (fair) laws and regulations to govern its citizens. And citizens have an obligation to

obey and respect these laws. Our Lord taught us the importance of recognizing civil authority when he was asked about the lawfulness of paying tribute to Caesar, "Render to Caesar the things that are Caesar's, and to God the things that are God's" (Lk 20:25). It is important to remember that in this passage Our Lord gives two commands. As Christians we must first of all obey the laws of God. Then, as citizens, we must obey the laws of society. Society, on the other hand, should promote citizens' exercise of virtue. It should foster appropriate values and establish the conditions for the proper exercise of freedom.

God's Laws Come First

Civil government is sometimes called "the state." The state, like every social organization, should protect and promote the dignity and rights of the human person. While the state has legitimate authority, it does not have the right to demand something which violates God's law. In order to exercise legitimate authority, the state must promote the common good through morally acceptable means. For example, no government has the right to command willful murder, since this is a violation of God's law. When such laws are made, citizens are not

bound to obey them. In fact, in some sense they are not really laws. In such a situation we should think of the words of St. Peter to the Sanhedrin, "We must obey God rather than men" (Acts 5:29).

To illustrate this point—that God's law is above the law of the state—we can look at the life of St. Thomas More. Thomas More was a great lawyer and statesman in England at the beginning of the sixteenth century. He was a layman who dedicated himself to serving his country and his king. He rose to prominence during the reign of his friend King Henry VIII and was eventually appointed Chancellor of England, second in power to the king.

In order to divorce his wife, King Henry declared himself to be the supreme head of the Church in England. All of his subjects were then required to take an oath acknowledging this and declaring their primary allegiance to the king. Thomas More knew that he could not take this oath, for that would mean denying God's law.

On July 6, 1535, Thomas More was beheaded—by order of the king and his court— for refusing to sign the oath. Before he died, he reminded us that God's law is supreme: "I die the king's good servant, but God's first."

Civil Laws

Although we are not bound to obey such unjust laws, we are bound to obey all laws which conform to God's laws. For example, we must obey laws regarding the property rights of others. In addition to obeying just laws, there are several other duties which we have as citizens.

As citizens we must develop the virtue of **patriotism**, which is love of one's country. It is natural and good for us to love our native land. Patriotism is not merely the emotional reaction we may have when we sing our na-

tional anthem or see our nation's flag. This emotional reaction may be the beginning. However, patriotism is actually a deep love for our country which prompts us to dedicate ourselves to promoting those things which are good for our country and its citizens.

At the same time, we must avoid that excessive love of country which can result in the error of excessive *nationalism*. This can result from a love which is blind to the defects of one's nation. One must also avoid the opposite error which is a lack of love for one's country which can lead one to despise and turn against one's own country. The actual betrayal of one's country is known as *treason*.

The Christian citizen must use his influence to help make his nation just. This is an area in which the laity are especially called to bring Christ to the world. We must work to promote just and moral laws, in keeping with God's law. When there are unjust laws, we must work to change them. We must work to change harmful attitudes such as racism and lack of respect for human beings, including the unborn and the poor, by conforming our own attitudes to justice, truth, and love. In a democratic nation, the Christian, then, has a particular duty to take part in the government of his country—voting for good leaders or perhaps even running for office himself.

Duties of Citizens

There are also other duties which we have as citizens. We must support the government through the payment of taxes and we should, if necessary, be willing to defend our country against unjust aggression. Finally, as Christians we have a particular obligation to pray for our leaders and our country.

Besides being citizens of our nation, we are also members of the larger society of the world. We cannot isolate ourselves in our own nation, but we must be concerned about all peoples. As Christians we have a responsibility to serve others—particularly those whose rights and human needs are not recognized. We must work for peace and justice in the world, practicing the corporal works of mercy wherever we can. Aside from the common good of a particular society, there is also a universal common good of the whole human family. This good requires an organization of the community of nations, which respects and promotes the rights of all peoples.

The Christian View of Creatures

In the first chapter of Genesis we read of the creation of the world. Out of nothing God brought into existence all the creatures of our world. First he created many inanimate objects —the sun, the moon, the mountains, and the seas. Then he made the various plants and the many animals—birds, fish, insects, and the beasts of the earth. Finally, as the pinnacle of his creation on earth, God created man and woman and said to them:

> Fill the earth and subdue it; and have dominion over the fish of the sea and over the birds of the air and over every living thing that moves upon the earth (Gen 1:28).

When God created the world he gave human beings *dominion* over his creation. This means that God made the earth and all of the creatures on it—animals, plants, mountains, rivers, etc.—for us. They were made, first of all, to glorify God and to remind us of him and lead us to himself—as does, for example, a magnificent sunset. But these things were also made to give us joy.

Because we are the highest creatures on earth, we have been entrusted with a great responsibility to exercise **stewardship** over creation. This means that we must take care of creation and use wisely the many gifts God has given us. We must not waste or abuse any of God's creation. We should care for creation so that future generations can share in what God has given us. Man depends on air, water, forests, plants, and animals for his life, food, and clothing. Stewardship does not mean that we cannot kill animals for these purposes, but we must use them for our needs, not wastefully. Nor should we cause animals any unnecessary suffering but treat them kindly.

St. Francis of Assisi can be an example for us of the care we should have for all God's creatures. Francis loved not only the poor of this world but all of God's creatures as well—animals and all of nature. He saw all of creation as traces and reflections of God. His tenderness for and his gentle sway over animals were often noted by his companions. He spoke of animals and indeed, all creatures, as his "brothers" and "sisters." His beautiful "Canticle of the Sun" illustrates this reverence for God's work.

Words to Know:
common good   patriotism
stewardship

"Let every person be subject to the governing authorities. For there is no authority except from God, and those that exist have been instituted by God. . . . for he [in authority] is God's servant for your good."

(Rom 13:1–4)

Q. 119 *Why must we obey those in authority?*

We must obey those in authority because this authority comes from God, and to oppose it is to oppose the authority of God (CCC 2197, 2234, Rom 13:1–2).

Q. 120 *What is the duty of a citizen?*

The duty of a citizen is to contribute to the common good in a spirit of truth, justice, solidarity, and freedom. We are to love and serve the community, pay taxes, vote, and defend our country (CCC 2239–40).

Q. 121 *What must we do if those in authority command us to violate God's law?*

If those in authority command us to violate God's law, we must obey God rather than men (CCC 2242, Acts 5:29).

CHAPTER 21

Law and Conscience

They show that what the law requires is written on their hearts, while their conscience also bears witness and their conflicting thoughts accuse or perhaps excuse them.

Romans 2:15

"The law is holy, and the commandment is holy and just and good" (Rom 7:12).

When we look at the world we see that everything operates according to a certain plan or order. For example, rivers flow toward the sea, birds build nests each spring for their young, and when we drop a stone it falls to the ground. As Creator of the world, God has provided for all of his creatures. In his *providence* he governs all things, directing and ordering each to its proper end or purpose. This is the **eternal law** of God which encompasses all creatures on earth.

The chart on page 136 shows that all laws come from God, the Eternal Law. Let us examine each of these sorts of law.

Physical Laws

God's eternal law is first divided into *physical laws* and *moral laws*. Physical laws, also called *laws of nature*, are those which govern the nature and operation of all material things and natural forces. The law of gravity or other laws of physics and chemistry are examples of physical laws. The instincts of animals, which cause them to act in particular ways, are also

physical laws. The laws which govern the physical world can neither be disobeyed nor repealed.

The laws which direct our will toward the good are called **moral laws**. Since human beings have free wills, the laws which guide our actions can be broken. We are always free to choose good or evil. Such laws help us to direct our wills toward their proper purpose—perfection on earth and, finally, happiness in heaven.

Blessed are those whose way is blameless, who walk in the law of the Lord! . . . who also do no wrong, but walk in his ways! (Ps 119:1, 3).

The entire moral law comes to us from God. Part of it comes directly from him, but another part of it comes indirectly from him through a human lawgiver. The first part, **divine law**, is divided into two sorts—*natural law* and *revealed law*.

Divine Law

Natural Law

The **natural law** is the basic moral law which God has placed in human nature and which we discover through reason. This law is written in the hearts of men, and its most basic principle is "Do good and avoid evil." However, because of original sin, which has clouded our intellects, we do not always recognize what is good and what is evil. Most people, even pagans, can easily see that certain things, like murder, stealing, or lying are wrong. However, it is not so easy to see that at times it can be wrong to say something which is actually true. For example, spreading facts that would deliberately harm or embarrass another person might be seriously wrong.

Revealed Law

Because human beings often find it difficult to know what is right and wrong on their own, God has also revealed certain commandments to us. This is what we call *positive* or *revealed law*. These are the commandments which are contained in the Old Law given through Moses at Mount Sinai and the New Law given by Our Lord when he was on earth. The Old Law was given by God in the Old Testament—for example, the Ten Commandments. This law was the first stage of God's revelation and by itself is incomplete. This law was perfected in the New Testament. Our Lord said: "Think not that I have come to abolish the law and the prophets; I have come not to abolish them but to fulfill them" (Mt 5:17). Our Lord tells us to keep his law out of love rather than out of fear (Jn 14:15). While the Ten Commandments are examples of revealed laws given in the Old Testament, the forbidding of divorce by Jesus (Mt 19:1–9) is an example of a revealed law from the New Testament. It is important to recall that the Church's magisterium is the authentic interpreter of divine law, that is, of both the natural law and positive revealed law.

Many of the revealed precepts repeat and confirm points in the natural law which men might discover on their own. God repeats these —for example, "Thou shalt not kill," "Thou shalt not steal"—because of their importance. Other precepts require God's revelation if we are to know them. Thus, for example, God tells us that we are to worship him on a particular day each week.

Human Laws

Many moral laws are made by humans themselves and are called *human laws*. Human laws are divided into *civil laws* and *ecclesiastical* (Church) *laws*. **Civil laws** are those made by the civil authorities. Laws regarding the payment of taxes or traffic laws are examples.

Ecclesiastical laws are those made by the Church. There are many ecclesiatical laws, and they are contained in the book of Canon

Church Teaching

". . . In forming their consciences the faithful must pay careful attention to the sacred and certain teaching of the Church. For the Catholic Church is, by the will of Christ, the teacher of truth. It is her duty to proclaim and teach with authority the truth which is Christ and, at the same time, to declare and confirm by her authority the principles of the moral order which spring from human nature itself" (DH, 14).

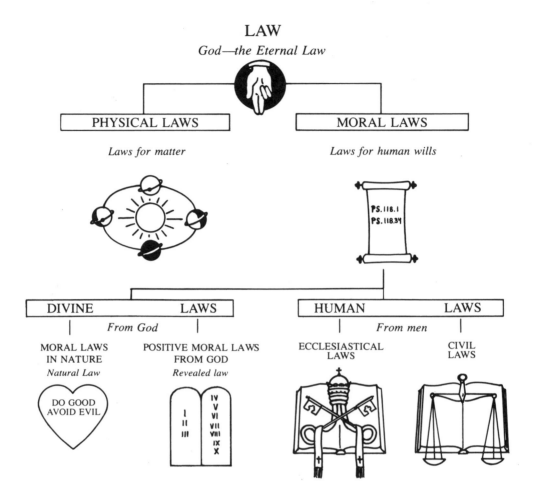

LAW

God—the Eternal Law

PHYSICAL LAWS	MORAL LAWS
Laws for matter	*Laws for human wills*

PS.118.1
PS.118.34

DIVINE LAWS		HUMAN LAWS	
From God		*From men*	
MORAL LAWS IN NATURE	POSITIVE MORAL LAWS FROM GOD	ECCLESIASTICAL LAWS	CIVIL LAWS
Natural Law	*Revealed law*		

DO GOOD AVOID EVIL

I II III IV V VI VII VIII IX X

Law. They are particularly important for all Catholics and we should know them. These are the precepts of the Church:

Precepts of the Church

1. "You shall attend Mass on Sundays and on holy days of obligation and rest from servile labor." The first precept requires us to keep holy the day of the Lord's Resurrection; to worship God by participating in Mass every Sunday and holy day of obligation; to avoid those activities that would hinder renewal of soul and body on the Lord's day.

2. "You shall confess your sins at least once a year." The second precept requires us to lead a sacramental life; to receive the Sacrament of Penance regularly—minimally, to receive the Sacrament of Penance at least once a year (annual confession is obligatory only if serious sin is involved) in preparation to receive Holy Communion.

3. "You shall receive the Sacrament of the Eucharist at least during the Easter Season." The third precept requires us to receive Holy Communion frequently; minimally, to receive Holy Communion once during the Easter Season.

4. "You shall observe the days of fasting and abstinence established by the Church." The fourth precept requires us to do penance, including abstaining from meat and fasting from food on the appointed days.

5. "You shall help to provide for the needs of the Church." The fifth precept requires us to strengthen and support the Church—one's own parish community and parish priests, the worldwide Church, and the Pope.

(CCC 2042–43)

Sometimes the government and the Church repeat and reaffirm divine laws. For example, a state may have laws against murder or stealing, and the Church also teaches us that these actions are wrong. Such laws, though repeated by men, are *not* human laws. They are *divine laws*. It is important to understand this because these laws cannot be changed by men.

We must also realize that there is a hierarchy among laws; for example, God's laws are higher than man's. Thus if a law of man is in conflict with or contradicts a law of God, we must follow God's law. This was what Thomas More did, as we saw in the last chapter.

When we speak of laws we speak of both the *spirit* and the *letter* of the law. The spirit is the understanding behind the law and the letter is the actual words of the law. In following these laws we must follow both the spirit and the letter.

There is a clear difference between the law and legalism. Christ said, "It is easier for heaven and earth to pass away, than for one dot of the law to become void" (Lk 16:17). On the other hand, he severely rebuked the Pharisees for their legalism. They had forgotten all about the spirit behind the law, while holding fast to the letter. Thus they made the law void. For instance, there was a tradition among them that

if you said to your parents that you were dedicating your goods to God, then you were no longer obliged to help and honor them. Jesus said, "So for the sake of your tradition, you have made void the word of God. You hypocrites! Well did Isaiah prophesy of you, when he said: 'This people honors me with their lips, but their heart is far from me' " (Mt 15:6–9). Time and again Christ showed that the law of charity is supreme. It does not void the law but fulfills it. St. Paul reminds us: "Above all these put on love" (Col 3:14).

Conscience

Besides the external guide of the moral law, God has also given us an internal guide to help us determine which actions are good and which are bad. This is known as our **conscience**. Many of us may think of our conscience as a 'little voice'—like Jiminy Cricket—which tells us what to do or scolds us when we do wrong.

This is a false understanding of conscience.

Conscience is a specific action of our reason, or intellect, by which we judge the rightness or wrongness of a particular action. It is not a feeling or emotion. Conscience is the application of certain principles—found in the moral law—to a specific, concrete moral situation.

In order to be of any use to us, our conscience must be correctly *formed* or taught. We are obliged to follow our conscience, but we are also obliged to make sure that our conscience is properly formed.

When our conscience is correctly formed and the judgments which we make are correct, we have a *true* conscience. If our judgments are incorrect we have a *false* conscience. A false conscience is lax if it fails to see sin where sin actually exists. For example, our conscience is lax if we do not think deliberately missing Mass on Sunday is a serious sin. A false conscience is scrupulous if it magnifies the gravity of sin or finds sin where there really is none. For example, our conscience is scrupulous if we think that missing Sunday Mass when we are very ill is a sin. Such false consciences have not been correctly formed.

To form our conscience we must look to the Church, which speaks the Word of God to us today, and we must listen to her voice. At the same time we should try to understand these laws of God so that we may be better able to follow them.

Words to Know:
eternal law   moral law   divine law
natural law   civil law
ecclesiastical law   conscience

Q. 122 *What is mortal sin?*
Mortal sin is an act of disobedience to the law of God in a serious matter, done with full knowledge and deliberate consent (CCC 1857).

Q. 123 *Why is serious deliberate sin called "mortal"?*
Serious deliberate sin is called mortal because it takes divine grace away from the soul, which is its life, and it makes the soul worthy of everlasting punishment and eternal death in hell (CCC 1855, 1861).

Q. 124 *What is venial sin?*

Venial sin is an act of disobedience to the law of God in a lesser matter, or in a matter that is serious, but done without full knowledge or consent (CCC 1862).

Q. 125 *What is an occasion of sin?*

An occasion of sin is any person, circumstance, or thing that puts us in danger of sinning (CCC 1865–69).

Q. 126 *Are we obliged to avoid the occasions of sin?*

Yes, we are obliged to avoid the occasions of sin because we are obliged to avoid sin itself (CCC 1451).

Q. 127 *Why does the Church have the authority to make laws and precepts?*

The Church has the authority to make laws and precepts because she has received this authority from Jesus Christ through his apostles (CCC 2035–38).

Q. 128 *Must the members of the Church obey the precepts of the Church?*

Yes, members of the Church must obey the precepts of the Church (CCC 2037).

Q. 129 *What is conscience?*

Conscience is the use of the reason or intellect in a person to judge the rightness or wrongness of an action. It is the application of certain principles (in the moral law) and must be formed correctly, for man is obliged to follow it (CCC 1777–78, 1783).

CHAPTER 22

The Church and the Social Order

For God sent the Son into the world, not to condemn the world, but that the world might be saved through him.

John 3:17

Immediately before the Ascension, Our Lord stood on the mountain in Galilee and said these words to his apostles: "Go therefore and make disciples of all nations, baptizing them in the name of the Father and of the Son and of the Holy Spirit, teaching them to observe all that I have commanded you. . ." (Mt 28:19–20). This final command tells us of the duty to spread the gospel to every man. But Our Lord meant more than baptizing individuals. He told the apostles to baptize all nations. This means to infuse society with the message of the gospel —to *form Christian nations.*

The Church's duty then extends beyond drawing individuals to Christ. The Church must also help to shape society so that the public morality will be Christian. In this way the Church "baptizes" the social order, so that all things may be renewed in Christ.

In Scripture we find mentioned four sins which "cry to heaven for vengeance." They are sodomy (perverse sexual behavior), willful murder, oppression of the poor, and defrauding the laborer of his just wage. These sins do not "cry to heaven" because they are the most serious sins. Idolatry and blasphemy, for ex-

ample, are even worse. These four sins, however, are all injustices which undermine the fundamental order of society—particularly the family, the basic unit of society. Because of their effect on society, the Church, over the centuries, has often addressed these matters in her social teachings.

Much of the Church's social teaching may be found in the *encyclicals* of the popes. These letters addressed to all the bishops and the entire Church are also a means of instructing the world and bringing the gospel to all nations. As we consider the last three of the sins which cry out to heaven, we will mention some of these encyclicals. Because they are addressed to the entire Church, they were written originally in the universal language of the Church — Latin. Below, the Latin title of each encyclical is given with the English title in parentheses.

Protection of Human Life

"Cain rose up against his brother Abel, and killed him. Then the Lord said to Cain, 'Where is Abel your brother? . . .

What have you done? The voice of your brother's blood is crying to me from the ground' " (Gen 4:8–10).

Murder was the first sin committed after the Fall. God, in speaking to Cain, tells us of the grave injustice which has been done. Yet, we know that not all killing is necessarily wrong. If Abel had killed Cain in self-defense this would not have been murder. Murder is the unjust taking of innocent life, which is what Cain did. This is also what is meant by the Fifth Commandment "Thou shalt not kill."

In modern times one of the most serious forms of willful murder is the killing of unborn children in the wombs of their mothers—**abortion**. This is the destruction of the most innocent and helpless human life. It destroys the future of our families and society. Abortion is certainly a sin which cries out to heaven.

Through her teachings the Church has always tried to protect human life from such injustices. During the twentieth century, when the practice of abortion spread to many nations—including our own—the popes frequently addressed the world on this matter. They have proclaimed the sacredness of human life from conception until natural death and the importance of the family, where new life begins and is nurtured. Three important social encyclicals which speak on these matters are *Casti Connubii* (Christian Marriage) by Pope Pius XI, *Humanae Vitae* (Of Human Life) by Pope Paul VI, and *Evangelium Vitae* (The Gospel of Life) by Pope John Paul II.

War and Peace

The Church has always taught that just as it is licit for a person to defend himself or his family or defenseless persons against attack, so it is licit for nations to defend themselves or help others defend themselves against unjust aggression. This is what is known as a **just war**. Of course, first, other avenues for stopping the attack must be considered and used, if possible and effective. Also, the response to an attack must not be out of proportion. The moral principle used is: "preserving the moderation of blameless defense."

The Second Vatican Council taught:

> Every act of war directed to the indiscriminate destruction of whole cities or vast areas with their inhabitants is a crime against God and man, which merits firm and unequivocal condemnation (GS, 80).

As far as nuclear deterrence is concerned Pope John Paul II stated that:

> under present conditions, deterrence based on equilibrium—certainly not as an end in itself, but as a stage on the way to progressive disarmament—can still be judged to be morally acceptable. How-

---

Church Teaching

"The Church makes a judgment about economic and social matters when the fundamental rights of the person or the salvation of souls requires it. She is concerned with the temporal common good of men because they are ordered to the sovereign Good, their ultimate end" (CCC, 2458).

ever, to insure peace it is indispensable not to be content with a minimum which is always fraught with a real danger of explosion (Message to the United Nations, June 1982).

Several national bishops' conferences have issued Pastoral Letters on the question of war and peace, for instance, the U.S. bishops and the French bishops. They agree on the basic principles, but also agree that the practical application may differ because prudential judgments are involved. Unjust war is contrary to God's plan for the human family. God's will is that men ought to be united among themselves. Indeed, there is a similarity between the unity of the three Persons in God and the unity God wills men to establish among themselves.

Social Justice

"You shall not wrong a stranger or oppress him . . . you shall not afflict any widow or orphan. If you do afflict them, and they cry out to me, I will surely hear their cry. . . (Ex 22:21–23).

"Behold, the wages of the laborers who mowed your fields, which you kept back by fraud, cry out; and the cries of the harvesters have reached the ears of the Lord . . ." (James 5:4)

Justice means giving a person what is due to him. Social justice means establishing conditions in society that allow individuals and groups to obtain their due. Such conditions require respect for the human person and for the rights that come from human dignity. This includes the basic equality of all human beings as being made in God's image.

The material goods of this worlds were given to man by God. Every human being should have what is necessary to live a decent human life.

Oppressing the poor, the widowed, the orphaned, etc., and defrauding the laborer of his wage are also sins which directly harm society. These two evils are the basis of the Church's teaching on economic and civic matters. The Church reminds all people and nations of their obligations in justice to care for the unfortunate among us. Almsgiving to the poor expresses the charity that God expects of his followers. Almsgiving is also an act of justice that pleases God. Thus, the Church teaches us of the evils of economic systems that exploit the poor. Human dignity requires that we try to eliminate sinful, excessive economic and social inequalities.

The Church also teaches us of the importance of paying the laborer a fair wage. Families cannot survive unless the heads of households are paid enough to provide for their basic needs—food, clothing, and shelter. The moral law also forbids enslaving human beings, or buying and selling human beings like merchandise. The basic equality of all men means that all men are to be respected as other "selves."

These teachings on economic issues have been particularly emphasized during the last one hundred years. The popes have written a number of important encyclicals on these topics. The first, in 1891, which is the basis for all those which followed, was *Rerum Novarum* (The Condition of Labor) by Pope Leo XIII. A more recent one, called *Laborem Exercens* (The Dignity of Labor), was written by Pope John Paul II.

In our concern for the promotion of the dignity of man, we must note that not every movement, ideology, or form of government which claims to benefit man or the poor does so. Certain movements in the twentieth century have been condemned by the Church. Communism, while claiming to be for the oppressed classes in society, actually exploits them and suppresses basic human rights. National Socialism (Nazism) claimed the superiority of one race, and the Nazis brutally enslaved and persecuted others, even committing mass genocide. Any form of racism is condemned by the Church, since we are all created in God's image and Christ died for each one of us. Consequently, the Church has taught about the evils of these systems. Pope Pius XI wrote two encyclicals on these matters—*Mit Brennender Sorge* (Against the Nationalist State) and *Divini Redemptoris* (On Atheistic Communism).

These social teachings remind us of our Christian call to live in the world without adopting the ways of the world. At various times in history, people have ignored the Church's guidance and lived in ways contrary to the gospel. Our task is to reshape the values of society, if we can. At all times, even if the world is against us, we must listen to and follow the Church.

Words to Know:
 just war   abortion

Q. 130 *Is all human life sacred?*
Yes, all human life is sacred and must be protected from conception to natural death (CCC 2270, 2277).

Q. 131 *What is the goal of social justice?*
The goal of social justice is for man to live in justice and peace according to divine wisdom (CCC 2419).

Q. 132 *Is war always forbidden?*
No, war is not always forbidden. All are obliged to work for avoidance of war, but some wars are just (CCC 2307–8, 2312).

PART THREE

The Means to Fulfill
Our Call to Holiness

CHAPTER 23

Prayer

Likewise the Spirit helps us in our weakness; for we do not know how to pray as we ought, but the Spirit himself intercedes for us with sighs too deep for words.

Romans 8:26

As Christians we are called to sanctify our lives and unite ourselves with Christ. The two principal means for accomplishing this are *prayer* and the *sacraments*.

Prayer is the lifting up of our minds and hearts to God. Just as the spoken word is our way of communicating with friends, so prayer is our way of conversing with God. Every thought of God—short or long—can be a prayer. We are called to "Pray at all times in the Spirit, with all prayer and supplication" (Eph 6:13). For example, we might acknowledge the sovereignty of God or express gratitude to him for blessings he has given us. Or we might simply express our love for him. All of these are prayers.

Prayer is essential to our spiritual lives, as we can see from the Gospels. During his public life Our Lord often prayed. For example, he prayed in the desert before beginning his public ministry, he prayed on the mountain before he was transfigured, and he prayed in the Garden of Gethsemane on the night before he died. By these actions he taught us the importance of prayer.

I beseech you, O Lord, that the fiery and honey-sweet strength of your love

may free my soul from all that is under heaven, that I may die out of love for you, who deigned to die out of love for me. *Amen.*

Prayer of St. Francis

But Jesus did not only teach us by example; he frequently spoke to the apostles about the necessity of prayer. At one point he told the apostles that they ". . . ought always to pray and not lose heart" (Lk 18:1). Here he told us that we need to pray—even when it is difficult. There are times, for example, when various thoughts may distract us from our prayer. Such distractions may discourage us and tempt us to quit, but Jesus tells us that we should continue. Although these distractions are not always our fault, we should still work to draw our thoughts back to God as a sign of our love for him.

How should we pray? First, before we pray we should *prepare* ourselves to turn our thoughts to God. We should try to dismiss all other thoughts from our minds and direct our attention to God. Sometimes visible reminders —such as statues or paintings—will help us to concentrate on God. Next, we should pray with *humility*, like the tax collector in one of

147

the parables told by Jesus (Lk 18:9–14). In addition, we should have *faith* and *confidence* that God will hear our prayer. As Our Lord said to his disciples at the Last Supper:

> Truly, truly, I say to you, if you ask anything of the Father, he will give it to you in my name (Jn 16:23).

Fourth, we should pray with *resignation* to the will of God, as Our Lord did on the eve of his death. That means that we accept how he answers our prayers. Finally, we should pray *with perseverance*. This means that we should keep on praying even if it seems as if God has not heard our prayer. To illustrate this point, Our Lord told the following parable:

> Which of you who has a friend will go to him at midnight and say to him, "Friend, lend me three loaves; for a friend of mine has arrived on a journey, and I have nothing to set before him"; and he will answer from within, "Do not bother me; the door is now shut, and my children are with me in bed; I cannot get up and give you anything"? I tell you, though he will not get up and give him anything because he is his friend, yet because of his importunity [persistence] he will rise and give him whatever he needs (Lk 11:5–8).

There are two forms of prayer—*mental* and *vocal*. **Mental prayer** is that which is said interiorly. Such prayer unites our hearts with God while we meditate on his holy truths. It usually begins with meditation—for example, on a passage from Scripture or one of the mysteries of our faith—which stirs our hearts to love God and unite ourselves with him. A good opportunity to pray in this manner is after we receive Our Lord in Holy Communion.

Vocal prayer is said by spoken words—alone or with others. However, the words alone are not prayer, as the prophet Isaiah reminded the people of the Old Testament:

> This people draw near with their mouth and honor me with their lips, while their hearts are far from me (Is 29:13).

We must join our hearts and minds to the words that we speak.

Vocal prayer may be *formal* or *informal*. Formal prayers are those that follow a set pattern or formula. These prayers use words composed by someone else—for example, Our Lord, the angel Gabriel, or one of the saints. The Our Father, the Hail Mary, the Memorare, and the Act of Contrition are all examples of formal prayers. The Psalms of the Old Testament, written by David and inspired by God, are also formal prayers. There are many times when such prayers help us to communicate our thoughts to God. They show us how we ought to pray. They lift our minds and hearts and fill us with heavenly desires and right attitudes. These prayers also unite us with other members of the Body of Christ, who pray the same prayers.

At other times it is good to use our own words to pray. This is called informal prayer. It allows us to talk to God sincerely about ourselves, offering to him our particular joys and sorrows and asking him for the special help we need.

Prayers may be said for four reasons: adoration, thanksgiving, contrition, and petition. Prayers that primarily acknowledge God's greatness and our dependence on him are prayers of *adoration*. While all of our prayers should begin as prayers of praise, some, such as the *Sanctus* (Holy, Holy, Holy) of the Mass are solely prayers of adoration.

The second reason for prayer is to give thanks to God for the blessings he has given us. These are prayers of *thanksgiving*. We are reminded of the importance of giving thanks during each Mass. Before the Eucharistic Prayer the priest proclaims "Let us give thanks to the Lord our God," to which we reply, "It is right to give him thanks and praise."

Contrition is the third reason for prayer. In a prayer of contrition we acknowledge our sins and pray to obtain forgiveness from God. When we say the *Confiteor* (I Confess) at the beginning of Mass we are saying a prayer of contrition.

The last reason for prayer *is petition*. This is the most common prayer; in fact, many people only remember to pray to God when they need something. Prayers of petition are those in which we ask God for blessings for ourselves and others. It is fitting that we should ask for God's help, since we do need it for our life on earth and in order to reach heaven. The *Prayers of the Faithful* during Mass are examples of prayers of petition.

Let us now consider some of the formal prayers that are important in the Catholic Church.

First in importance are those prayers that are part of the Church's liturgy—the Mass and the Liturgy of the Hours. The Mass is the perfect prayer, because it is the offering of Christ to his Father in heaven. The Mass is also the supreme act of worship, by which we thank God. Because the Mass is the same sacrifice as that of Calvary, it is the perfect means of making satisfaction for our sins. Since the Mass is in memory of the Resurrection, it is a prayer of thanksgiving. Finally, since the Mass is the perfect sacrifice, it is the best way of petitioning God.

The Liturgy of the Hours is also an important prayer. It is a prayer of praise, by which we can sanctify our entire day. As we have seen, certain members of the Church—priests and religious—are required to pray the **Divine Office** each day. But we also are invited by the Church to join in this prayer.

One day the disciples said to Jesus, "Lord, teach us to pray," and he taught them the *Our Father*, or *Lord's Prayer*. This prayer contains an outline of all the qualities that should be present in our prayers and all those things that we should ask of God. Hence, it is not just a wonderful prayer, it is also a model for all of our prayers. It is so rich in meaning that we could meditate on it all our lives. Let us briefly examine the statements found in the Our Father.

Our Father, who art in heaven,

We begin this prayer by placing ourselves in the presence of God, recognizing him as our Father, but also as God.

hallowed be thy name,

Next we adore God, as we ask that his name be made holy and honored on earth.

thy Kingdom come,

We pray that his Kingdom—the Kingdom of Christ, the Church—may grow and be spread throughout the earth.

thy will be done on earth as it is in heaven

We end the first half of this prayer asking that God's will—not ours—be done. To all three of these first petitions we add "*on earth as it is in heaven,*" for God's name is honored in heaven; in heaven his Kingdom has been spread; and finally, in heaven his will is done.

Give us this day our daily bread,

We pray now for ourselves, asking God to give us the things we need—both physical and spiritual.

and forgive us our trespasses as we forgive those who trespass against us.

We acknowledge our sins and ask that God in his mercy forgive us in the same measure as we have forgiven those who offend us.

Lead us not into temptation, but deliver us from evil.

We end the prayer asking God to help us in times of temptation and to strengthen us when we face occasions of sin.

Another great prayer that the Church especially recommends is the *Rosary*. This prayer has been part of the spiritual life of many Catholics—mainly in the Latin rite—for about eight centuries. The Church has encouraged us to say this beautiful prayer by dedicating one month—October—to the Rosary. The Rosary combines both mental and vocal prayer. It is divided into fifteen mysteries, or episodes, from the lives of Jesus and Mary. As we recite the vocal prayers—one Our Father, ten Hail Marys, and one Glory Be for each mystery—we meditate on the various events from the lives of Our Lord and his Mother.

It is important to develop times for prayer in our lives, so that we may fulfill our call to holiness. In the next chapter we will consider the sacraments that further nourish our spiritual life.

Words to Know:
mental prayer   vocal prayer
Divine Office

Q. 133 *What is prayer?*

Prayer is the lifting of the mind and heart to God, in order to know him better, to adore him, to thank him, and to ask him for what we need (CCC 2559, 2590).

Q. 134 *How many forms of prayer are there?*

There are two forms of prayer: mental and vocal (CCC 2700–24).

Q. 135 *What is mental prayer?*

Mental prayer is that which is offered with the mind and heart alone (CCC 2708).

Q. 136 *What is vocal prayer?*

Vocal prayer is that prayer which is expressed by spoken words with the participation of the mind and heart (CCC 2700).

Q. 137 *How should we pray?*

We should pray humbly, attentively, and devoutly (CCC 2559).

Q. 138 *Why is it necessary to pray?*

It is necessary to pray in order to grow in our faith in God, in our hope in him, and in our love for him, and in this way to receive the grace necessary to be united with him in heaven (CCC 2558).

CHAPTER 24

The Sacramental Life

But one of the soldiers pierced his side with a spear, and at once there came out blood and water.

John 19:34

In addition to prayer, Christ has given us a wonderful means to become holy. The *sacraments* were given to the Church by Jesus Christ to sanctify us. They are the means by which we receive the "living water" of which Our Lord spoke. Water in this sense signifies the life of God called *sanctifying grace*.

A **sacrament** is an outward sign instituted by Christ to give us grace. A *sign* is a thing that stands for, or represents, something else. For example, our national flag represents our country; smoke indicates the presence of fire. We are all familiar with the signs in the sacraments. The water in Baptism, for example, indicates our death to sin, the cleansing of the soul, and the new life which is given by God. But the sacraments are more than ordinary signs. They are *efficacious* signs. This means that they actually bring about what they represent.

To understand this better, think about the ordinary stop sign. This sign indicates to the driver that he should stop at an intersection. But it cannot *make* him stop; he must stop himself. The sacraments are different. In Baptism when the water is poured and the words "I baptize you . . ." are spoken, the soul is actually cleansed and the new life of **grace** is actually infused. This is the great power that Our Lord gave to these simple signs.

Christ himself gave us the sacraments so that we could share in his life and have that life nourished in us. He gave us these sacraments so that we would have a certain, or sure, way to receive the grace he won by dying on the Cross for us. But why did he choose to give us this grace through the sacraments?

As human beings we learn through *corporeal*, material, things around us. Thus, to learn we depend on our senses—sight, hearing, touch, taste, and smell. Our Lord gave us the sacraments as *sensible* means—means that can be sensed—for us to know that grace is active in our lives. At Baptism, when we see the water being poured and hear the words, we know that God's life now dwells in the soul of the person baptized. We are certain of this. In the same way, when we hear the priest in Confession say that our sins are forgiven, we *know* that God has forgiven our sins.

All of the sacraments make us holy by giving us grace or by restoring or increasing the life of grace in us. Thus all of the sacraments nourish and strengthen our spiritual life and help us draw closer to God. However, two of the sacraments are our "lifelines" to grace—Penance and the Holy Eucharist.

153

The Sacrament of Penance

On the evening of the Resurrection, Our Lord appeared to the apostles in the upper room. He said to them, "Receive the Holy Spirit. If you forgive the sins of any, they are forgiven; if you retain the sins of any, they are retained" (Jn 20:22–23). Christ gave the apostles and their successors the power to forgive sins, thus instituting the Sacrament of Penance, or Reconciliation.

Although original sin is removed through the sacrament of Baptism, we know that we are still in a weakened state. We have a strong inclination to sin, and we do, in fact, easily fall into sin. Our Lord knew that even after Baptism Christians could still sin. He gave us the Sacrament of Penance, or Reconciliation, so that we could receive God's forgiveness frequently.

The sacrament of Penance, then, is a great gift by which the sins we commit after Baptism are forgiven. If we have committed a mortal sin, God restores to our soul his life which had been lost. God increases his life within us and strengthens our friendship with him when we confess our venial sins. In addition, through the actual or sacramental graces which we receive, God helps us to avoid sin in the future. For example, if you confess that you have lied, God will give you strength and help you be truthful in the future.

The sacrament of Penance can help us draw closer to God and make us better and stronger Christians. For this reason, it is good to receive this sacrament often—even when we have not committed any mortal sins.

To make a good Confession and worthily receive the sacrament we must do five things:

1. Before receiving the sacrament you must examine your conscience. You should ask God to help you recognize your sins since your last confession.

2. You must have true sorrow, *contrition*, for your sins. This contrition is based on our love of God, sorrow for having offended him, and hatred of our sins.

3. You must have a firm commitment not to sin again. This means that you must resolve to do all you can to avoid sin and the occasions of sin in the future. If you do not intend to give up your sinful ways, God cannot forgive you. You would not be truly sorry.

4. You must confess your sins honestly to the priest. This means that you should not conceal any mortal sins. Neither should you try to hide anything out of shame or embarrassment. The priest, taking the place of Christ, is there to give you forgiveness and not to rebuke you unnecessarily. He may, however, give you some advice or guidance to help you overcome your sins.

5. You must be willing to perform the

"I am the bread of life; he who comes to me shall not hunger, and he who believes in me shall never thirst."

(John 6:35)

"... This is the bread which comes down from heaven, that a man may eat it and not die."

(John 6:50)

penance which the priest gives you and then to do it.

The Holy Eucharist

"Truly, truly, I say to you . . . he who eats my flesh and drinks my blood, has eternal life. . ." (Jn 6:53–54).

The **Eucharist** is the sacrament in which Our Lord is present—Body and Blood, Soul and Divinity—under the appearances of bread and wine. Just as our bodies need physical nourishment in order to live, our souls also must be nourished. The Eucharist is this spiritual food.

The Eucharist is a means of receiving grace and, at the same time, is the source of grace— Jesus, himself. The Eucharist is thus the most important sacrament and the fountain from which all grace flows.

In receiving the Eucharist—called Holy Communion—we become united to Christ. This union nourishes us by helping us to become more like Christ. Through reception of Communion the life of God is increased in our souls, bringing us closer to him. Just as food strengthens our bodies for difficult physical tasks, this great Sacrament helps us to become spiritually stronger.

To benefit from the graces of the Eucharist we must prepare ourselves to receive it worthily. These are the things we must do:

1. We must be in the state of grace when we receive Holy Communion. This means that if we have committed a mortal sin we must first go to Confession before receiving Our Lord. St. Paul told the Christians at Corinth: "Whoever . . . eats the bread or drinks the cup of the Lord in an unworthy manner will be guilty of profaning the body and blood of the Lord" (1 Cor 11:27). To receive Our Lord in the state of serious sin is a sin of sacrilege.

2. To receive the Eucharist worthily we must believe that Jesus Christ is truly present in the sacrament. Again St. Paul reminds us: ". . . anyone who eats and drinks without discerning the body eats and drinks judgment upon himself" (1 Cor 11:29). We must, then, prepare our-

---

Soul of Christ, sanctify me.
Body of Christ, save me.
Blood of Christ, inebriate me.
Water from the side of Christ,
     wash me.
Passion of Christ, strengthen me.
O Good Jesus, hear me.
Within thy wounds, hide me.
Suffer me not to be separated
     from thee.
From the malicious enemy,
     defend me.
In the hour of death, call me.
And bid me come to thee, that
     with thy saints I may praise
     thee for ever and ever. *Amen.*

> "According to the riches of his glory he may grant you to be strengthened with might through his Spirit in the inner man, and that Christ may dwell in your hearts through faith; that you, being rooted and grounded in love, may have power to comprehend with all the saints what is the breadth and length and height and depth, and to know the love of Christ which surpasses knowledge, that you may be filled with all the fulness of God."
>
> (Ephesians 3:16–19)

selves to receive Communion by remembering that we are about to receive the Body and Blood of Our Lord.

3. We must observe the Eucharistic fast. The Church gives us this law—no food or drink (except water or medicine) for one hour before receiving Communion —out of reverence so that we may prepare ourselves to receive our great Lord and King. This small sacrifice reminds us of what we are about to do. (The sick and those who care for them are exempt from this fast.)

4. After we receive Our Lord, we should spend time in *thanksgiving—thanking* him for coming to us and asking Jesus to help us. The following prayer, called the *Anima Christi*, might help us meditate on the great gift we receive. Many people recite this prayer after Communion.

Because the Eucharist is our source of spiritual nourishment, it is good to receive this sacrament frequently. By attending Mass each Sunday we are able to receive Holy Communion at least once a week. However, realizing the greatness of this sacrament, we should try to receive Our Lord even more often—even daily—by attending Mass during the week. St. Francis de Sales, in his *Introduction to the Devout Life* reminds us of this.

> Two classes of people should communicate often, the perfect because, being well prepared, they would be very wrong not to approach the fountainhead of perfection; and the imperfect, that they might preserve their strength; the weak that they might become strong; the sick that they might find a cure; the healthy, that they might be preserved from sickness.

Even when we are unable to attend Mass we can make a *spiritual communion* in which we ask Our Lord to come to us and dwell in us in a special way.

When we pray, "Give us this day our daily bread," we include asking to receive the Eucharist. When we realize the extreme love for us which Jesus showed in establishing a way to stay with us on earth, we will long to receive him as often as possible. He was the delight of the saints. St. Teresa of Avila prayed that "though our bodily eyes cannot feast themselves on the sight of him since he is hidden from us, he may reveal himself to the eyes of the soul and may make himself known to us as another kind of food, full of delight and joy, which sustains our life."

St. Bonaventure prays: "Grant that my soul may hunger after you . . . upon whom the angels desire to look, and may my inmost soul be filled with the sweetness of your savor; may it ever thirst for you, the fountain of life, the foundation of wisdom and knowledge, the fountain of eternal light, the torrent of pleasure, the richness of the house of God."

In addition to the reception of Our Lord in the Eucharist, we can adore him and draw closer to him through adoration of the Blessed Sacrament. The *Real Presence* of Christ in the Eucharist remains after Mass. Therefore consecrated Hosts are reserved in the tabernacle in the church. Because Christ is truly present in our churches and chapels, we should try to spend time adoring him, thanking him, and talking to him about our needs. If we cannot get to daily Mass, perhaps we can make a daily visit to Our Lord in the Blessed Sacrament.

Besides such visits, there are sometimes special devotions to the Blessed Sacrament in which we can participate. We may go to church for **Benediction**. The Eucharist is placed in a special container called a **monstrance**, so that we may see and adore the Body of Christ. The priest holds up the monstrance and blesses us with Christ himself. Sometimes the Host in the monstrance will be exposed on our altars for a period of time so that we may pray to Our Lord in a special way.

These devotions remind us of Christ's presence in the Eucharist and help us draw closer to him. We can deepen our union with Christ by receiving Communion often and visiting him in the Blessed Sacrament.

Words to Know:

sacrament   grace   Eucharist
Benediction   monstrance

Prayer After Communion

"My Lord Jesus Christ, I believe that you are truly within me with your Body, Blood, soul and divinity; humbled in my nothingness, I adore you profoundly as my God and my Lord."

"... Whoever drinks of the water that I shall give him will never thirst; the water that I shall give him will become in him a spring of water welling up to eternal life."

(Jn 4:14)

Q. 139 *What are sacraments?*

Sacraments are outward signs instituted by Jesus Christ to give us grace and to make us holy (CCC 1115–16).

Q. 140 *What are the seven sacraments?*

The seven sacraments are Baptism, Confirmation, Holy Eucharist, Penance, Anointing of the Sick, Holy Orders, and Matrimony (CCC 1113).

Q. 141 *What is the Sacrament of Penance?*

The Sacrament of Penance (also called confession and reconciliation) is the sacrament instituted by Jesus Christ to forgive those sins committed after Baptism (CCC 1425).

Q. 142 *What five things are required to make a good confession?*

The five things required to make a good confession are: 1) examination of conscience; 2) contrition; 3) the intention not to sin again; 4) the accusation of our sins to a priest; 5) reception of absolution and penance (CCC 1451, 1454–55, 1459).

Q. 143 *How is an examination of conscience made?*

An examination of conscience is made by recalling the sins we have committed in thought, word, act, or omission against the Commandments of God, against the Precepts of the Church, or against the obligations to our state in life, since our last good confession (CCC 1454).

Q. 144 *In the examination of conscience should we seek to know the number of our mortal sins?*

In the examination of conscience we should seek with diligence to know the number of our mortal sins (CCC 1456).

Q. 145 *What is contrition?*

Contrition is sorrow of the soul and hatred for the sins we have committed, which brings us to form the intention not to sin again (CCC 1451–53).

Q. 146 *Is it necessary to have contrition for all the sins we have committed?*

It is necessary to have contrition for all the mortal sins we have committed, and it is fitting to have sorrow also for our venial sins (CCC 1452–53).

Q. 147 *When is it fitting to do the penance given in the Sacrament of Penance?*

It is fitting to do the penance given in the Sacrament of Penance as soon as possible, unless the confessor has assigned a particular time for it (CCC 1460).

Q. 148 *What effects does the Eucharist produce in him who receives it worthily?*

In him who receives it worthily, the Holy Eucharist produces and increases grace, the life of the soul, wipes away venial sins, preserves us from future mortal sin, and gives spiritual joy and consolation by increasing the hope of eternal life, of which it is the pledge (CCC 1392, 1394, 1402).

Q. 149 *What is transubstantiation?*

Transubstantiation is the change of bread and wine into the Body, Blood, Soul, and Divinity of our Lord Jesus Christ, which occurs at Consecration (CCC 1376).

Q. 150 *What sin does a peron commit if he deliberately receives Holy Communion in the state of mortal sin?*

Sacrilege is the sin a person commits who receives Holy Communion in the state of mortal sin (CCC 1385).

PART FOUR

The End of Christian Life

162

CHAPTER 25

Death and the Particular Judgment

"Truly, I say to you, today you will be with me in Paradise."

Luke 23:43

Each year on Ash Wednesday we hear the words: "Remember, man, that you are dust and to dust you will return" to remind us of our mortality. Each of us will eventually die. This is one of the consequences for all living, material creatures. Plants and animals eventually die; even inanimate, non-living, objects do not last for ever. Human beings, since we are mortal, must eventually die, a result of original sin.

Although the separation of body and soul—death—is inevitable, we know that there is life beyond the grave. Human beings have a mortal body but an *immortal* soul. **Immortal** means living forever. Because of this we see that death is not really the end of life but only the end of this life. In the Preface used at Masses for the dead we are reminded that for the Christian "life is not ended but merely changed."

Our faith tells us that death is the gateway to life with God. In the Gospel, Martha, the sister of Lazarus, showed us how Christians ought to understand death. When Our Lord came to Bethany after Lazarus' death, Martha said to Him: "I know that [my brother] will rise again in the resurrection at the last day" (Jn 11:24).

Since death will come for each of us, what should be our attitude toward it? Our Lord tells us that we should prepare ourselves for death. We should remember the parable about the servants who are awaiting their master's return. Since they do not know exactly when he will come, they must prepare themselves. We must also be prepared:

Watch therefore—for [you] do not know when the master of the house will come, in the evening, or at midnight, or at cockcrow, or in the morning. . . (Mk 13:35).

How can we prepare ourselves for death? We prepare throughout our lives by growing in faith and love. The best preparation for death is to live according to God's will, developing our spiritual lives through prayer and the sacraments. Whenever we pray the Hail Mary we ask our Mother in heaven to pray for us "now and at the hour of our death." Following our vocation and generously serving God will prepare us for death and our meeting with Christ.

"Everyone who sees the Son and believes in him should have eternal life and I will raise him up at the last day"

(John 6:40)

We should pray that we may receive the sacraments before our death. By the sacrament of Anointing, dangerously ill persons are commended to the Lord, that he may support and save them. Hopefully, we will also be able to receive the sacrament of Penance and the Eucharist as Viaticum.

When we die we will meet Our Lord and be judged by him. The **particular judgment** occurs at the moment of our death and will be based on those things which we did or neglected to do in this life. At this judgment we will see ourselves as we are—our sins and failings, as well as our virtues. We will also see the perfect justice of God's judgment. For this reason it is extremely important to develop the habit of appealing to God's mercy for us sinners. This appeal, made habitually, will bring down his mercy on us and others for that moment when we so critically need it. By remembering what St. Paul said we will prepare for this great moment:

> He will render to every man according to his works: to those who by patience in well-doing seek for glory and honor and immortality, he will give eternal life; but for those who are factious and do not obey the truth, but obey wickedness, there will be wrath and fury (Rom 2:6–8).

At the particular judgment those who have died in the state of mortal sin—without repenting—will be separated from God for ever. They will suffer eternal punishment because of their own actions and choice. In the parable of the rich man (Dives) and Lazarus Our Lord reminded us of the permanence of this state (Lk 16:19–31). Once one is in hell, there is no chance for repentance. While the souls of the damned suffer sensible pain, the greatest suffering in hell is the loss of God. They will be without hope, knowing that their own rejection of God is the cause of their damnation.

It is good to remember that God does not want anyone to suffer in hell. In fact, he did not create hell for man. The angels who rebelled were banished from God's sight and this is hell. God created man, like the angels, with a free will. Thus, if we should turn away from him, we will join the fallen angels in suffering this eternal punishment.

Some who die are not in the state of mortal sin, but still have venial sins which they have not fully repented of or done adequate penance for. Because these people have not completely separated themselves from God, they will not go to hell. They will go first to *purgatory*. Here they will be prepared for heaven. The doctrine of purgatory is very consoling since, because of God's mercy, we can be saved even though we are not perfect. We can go through a time of purification. Even though it is a painful suffering, we are full of hope.

Other people whose love for God is perfect will go straight to heaven. The reward for the just is *eternal life* in which they will enjoy the vision of God. This is called the **Beatific Vision**. In heaven "we shall see [God] as he is"

(1 Jn 3:2). It is this which gives us true happiness. In heaven, we will know God as completely as we can:

> Now we see in a mirror dimly, but then face to face. Now I know in part; then I shall understand fully. . . (1 Cor 13:12).

Here we will be able perfectly to love God and others.

We know that heaven will bring us great joy, and yet it is difficult for us to grasp what it is really like. St. Paul tells us:

> No eye has seen, nor ear heard, nor the heart of man conceived, what God has prepared for those who love him (1 Cor 2:9).

Heaven will be far greater than anything we can imagine. It will encompass all those things which are truly good.

Besides the great joy of the Beatific Vision, there will be other joys in heaven. In heaven there will be no sorrow or pain as St. John tells us in the book of Revelation:

> He will wipe away every tear from their eyes . . . neither shall there be mourning nor crying nor pain any more. . . (Rev 21:4).

There will also be no more sin or temptation in heaven. The struggle will be over and peace will remain. We will be united with the angels, the saints, and those we have known and loved on earth.

Since we cannot really understand much of what heaven is like, we may sometimes be tempted to think that it will be boring. Yet boredom is an imperfection of life on earth and cannot be part of life in heaven. If boredom is a part of life after death, it is part of life in hell, not heaven. Although the many particulars of life in heaven are unknown, we should remember the words of St. Paul—heaven is beyond our wildest dreams!

We should begin now by preparing ourselves for the day when Christ will call us to come home and be with him. We want to be able to say the words which St. Paul wrote near the end of his life, in a letter to Timothy:

> For I am already on the point of being sacrificed; the time of my departure has come. I have fought the good fight, I have finished the race, I have kept the faith. Henceforth there is laid up for me the crown of righteousness, which the Lord, the righteous judge, will award to me on that Day, and not only to me but also to all who have loved his appearing (2 Tim 4:6–8).

Words to Know:
immortal
particular judgment   Beatific Vision

Q. 151 *What is the Sacrament of the Anointing of the Sick?*

The Sacrament of the Anointing of the Sick is given to Christians who are gravely ill for their spiritual and bodily strengthening (CCC 1499).

Q. 152 *Who is the minister of the Sacrament of the Anointing of the Sick?*

The minister of the Sacrament of the Anointing of the Sick is a priest: the pastor of the parish or another priest who has his permission (CCC 1519).

Q. 153 *How does the priest administer the Sacrament of the Anointing of the Sick?*

The priest administers the Anointing of the Sick by anointing the forehead and the hands of the sick person with the oil blessed by the bishop or priest and by saying: "Through this holy anointing may the Lord in his love and mercy help you with the grace of the Holy Spirit. Amen. May the Lord, who frees you from sin, save you and raise you up. Amen." (CCC 1517–19).

Q. 154 *When can the Sacrament of the Anointing of the Sick be given?*

The Sacrament of the Anointing of the Sick can be given whenever a person is in a dangerous condition of health, either on account of an illness serious in itself, a serious injury, or on account of old age (CCC 1514).

Q. 155 *What happens to each of us at the end of life?*

At the end of life each of us will die, our body and soul will be separated, and we will face a particular judgment (CCC 1005, 1022).

Q. 156 *On what will Jesus Christ judge us?*

Jesus Christ will judge us on the good and evil that we have done in life, including our thoughts, and things we failed to do in response to God's grace (CCC 1021).

Q. 157 *What happens to each man after the particular judgment?*

After the particular judgment, those who love God and are perfectly holy go immediately to heaven to be with him. Those who love God but still need purification go to purgatory until they are ready to be with God in heaven. Those who have rejected God through dying in mortal sin go to hell (CCC 1022).

Q. 158 *What is hell?*

Hell is the eternal suffering of separation from God (CCC 1033–35).

Q. 159 *How long will heaven and hell last?*

Heaven and hell will last forever (CCC 1022, 1033).

CHAPTER 26

The Trumpet Shall Sound—
The End of the World

"Tell us, when will this be, and what will be the sign of your coming and of the close of the age?"

Matthew 24:3

At the Ascension of Our Lord into heaven, two angels spoke to the apostles saying:

"Why do you stand looking into heaven? This Jesus, who was taken up from you into heaven, will come in the same way as you saw him go into heaven" *(Acts 1:11).*

In the Nicene Creed we say that Jesus "will come again in glory to judge the living and the dead." When Christ first came among us, he came in poverty, humility, and weakness. He was born in a stable fit for animals, not a King. He was God, but he took on human nature and began his life in the most humble state—as a baby. He was God, but he took on the weaknesses of human nature—except sin—in order to teach us. When Christ comes again—the **Second Coming**—at the end of the world, he will come in triumph, as the King and Judge of the world. He will come in glory and be recognized by all men as Christ the King.

The time when this Second Coming will occur is unknown. When the apostles asked Our Lord about the end of the world (Mt 24), he spoke of various signs and warnings which would precede the event. He said that there would be wars and rumors of wars, famines, false prophets, and persecutions. All of these, however, have occurred at various times in history. And many individuals in the past (as well as the present) have mistaken the troubles of their own times as signs of the end of the world. But they neglected Our Lord's final words about the end, which are the most important:

But of that day and hour no one knows, not even the angels of heaven . . . the Father only. . . (Mt 24:36).

Just as we do not know when the world will end, we do not know exactly how it will end either. It is possible that the end of the world will be caused by humans, for example through war or the misuse of natural resources. But it is also possible that God will directly bring about the end of the world. However, it will not take place until God wills it.

At the end of the world Our Lord will judge the entire human race. This is known as the **General Judgment** and is described by Our Lord in the Gospel of Matthew (Mt 25). At that time Christ will judge both those who are alive at the end and those who have already died. All of our deeds—even secret ones—will be made known. Everyone will recognize the holiness of the just and understand why they have been rewarded. We will also see God's justice in the condemnation of unrepentant sinners who will be banished for eternity to hell. There will be no changes in the judgment for those who have already died. But now, however, their judgment will be made known to all.

The *Dies Irae* (which means "day of wrath") is a Latin poem which was written many centuries ago and sung on All Souls' Day and at Masses for the dead. It reminds us of this day of final judgment. Below are two verses which illustrate what will occur at the last judgment:

> Then the volume shall be spread
> And the writing shall be read
> Which shall judge the quick and dead.
> When the Judge his place has ta'en
> All things shall be made plain
> Nothing unavenged remain.

Those who have loved God and served him on this earth will stand on his right. They will be rewarded with heaven. Those who have turned away from God will stand on the left and will be banished for ever to hell. There will no longer be any need for purgatory at the end of the world. Those souls who are in purgatory at the end will go to heaven. All the wisdom, justice, mercy and loving kindness of God in his dealings with men will be made known. Our Lord Jesus Christ will be fully glorified. He will appear in splendor and triumph. Evil will be completely overcome. The reign of God will be complete.

> We shall not all sleep, but we shall all be changed, in a moment, in the twinkling of an eye, at the last trumpet. For the

trumpet will sound, and the dead will be raised imperishable, and we shall be changed. For this perishable nature must put on the imperishable, and this mortal nature must put on immortality (1 Cor 15:51–53).

At the end of the world, also, our human natures will once again be complete. Our bodies will be reunited with our souls, because man is both body and soul. This is called the *resurrection of the body*. We will enjoy the glories of heaven or suffer the pains of hell as a complete human being—body and soul.

The bodies of the just will be glorified in heaven. This means that our bodies will be perfected as was Our Lord's body after the Resurrection. Theologians have distinguished four properties or gifts which will belong to the glorified body. The glorified body will be incapable of physical suffering and will be free from death. This is known as *impassibility*, which comes from the Latin word "to suffer." Our bodies will have the property of *subtlety*, which means that our spiritual nature will shine through the body instead of being hidden by it. Thirdly, the glorified body will possess *agility*, which means that the body will be able to obey the soul with great ease and speed. This was manifested by the risen Christ, who quickly disappeared from the midst of the apostles (Jn 20:19, 26). Finally our resurrected bodies will have *clarity*. They will be free from all deformities—even minor ones—and will be filled with beauty.

Even the earth will be transformed in some way. St. John had a vision of the transformation of all things which he tells us in the book of Revelation:

Then I saw a new heaven and new earth; for the first heaven and the first earth had passed away, and the sea was no more. And I saw the holy city, new Jerusalem, coming down out of heaven from God . . . and I heard a great voice from the throne saying, "Behold, the dwelling of God is with men. He will dwell with them, and they shall be his people. . ." (Rev 21:1–3).

All of this is the perfect happiness which awaits us. God has prepared this for us. We must spend our lives preparing for this so that we may enjoy the blessings of heaven for eternity.

"When the Son of man comes in his glory, and all the angels with him, then he will sit on his glorious throne. Before him will be gathered all the nations. . . . Then the King will say to those on his right hand, 'Come, O blessed of my Father, inherit the kingdom prepared for you from the foundation of the world; for I was hungry and you gave me food, I was thirsty and you gave me drink, I was a stranger and you welcomed me, I was naked and you clothed me, I was sick and you visited me, I was in prison and you came to me.' . . . Then he will say to those on his left hand, 'Depart from me you cursed, into the eternal fire prepared for the devil and his angels; for I was hungry and you gave me no food, I was thirsty and you gave me no drink. . . .'"

(Matthew 25:31–36, 41–42)

Words to Know:
Second Coming   General Judgment

Q. 160 *Will Jesus Christ visibly return to earth?*

Yes, Jesus Christ will visibly return to earth to judge the living and the dead at the end of the world, at the General Judgment (CCC 671).

Q. 161 *What awaits us at the end of the world?*

The resurrection of the body and the General Judgment await us at the end of the world (CCC 678).

Q. 162 *Will Jesus Christ wait until the end of the world to judge us?*

Jesus Christ will not wait until the end of the world to judge us, he will judge each one of us immediately after death. This is called the particular judgment (CCC 1021–22).

Q. 163 *What does "resurrection of the body" mean?*

The "resurrection of the body" means that our bodies will be transformed by the power of God and reunited with our souls, so that we will share in the eternal reward or punishment we have merited (CCC 988, 997–98).

Appendix

WORDS TO KNOW

ABORTION: Deliberately killing an unborn child.

AGNOSTIC: One who holds that it is not possible to know whether God exists.

ANIMISM: The belief that inanimate objects possess supernatural powers and can be controlled by us.

ANNUNCIATION: God's announcement to Mary through the Archangel Gabriel that she was chosen to be the mother of the Son of God.

APOSTOLATE: Work carried out to help further the mission of Christ, after the example of the apostles.

APOSTOLIC: Connected with the apostles.

APOSTOLIC FATHERS: Early Christian saints whose writings have a special value because they witness to the teaching of the apostles.

ASSUMPTION: The taking up into heaven of the body and soul of Mary.

ATHEISTS: One who denies the existence of God.

BEATIFIC VISION: The direct vision of God experienced by the saints in heaven and which constitutes their perfect happiness.

BENEDICTION: A Eucharistic devotion of Roman Rite Catholics. It consists of hymns, readings from the Bible, and the blessing of the people with the Holy Eucharist. It is a way of worshipping God and affirming our belief in the Real Presence of Jesus in the Blessed Sacrament.

BISHOPS: Successors of the apostles who have received the fullness of the priesthood. Bishops are the spiritual leaders of Christians in their dioceses (geographical areas). They alone can ordain men to the priesthood and to the office of bishop. United with the Pope, they are the official teachers of the faith in the world.

CANONIZED SAINT: Someone whom the Church has officially declared to be in heaven.

CAPITAL SINS: Sins which engender other sins and vices. They are traditionally seven: pride, covetousness, envy, anger, gluttony, lust, and sloth.

CARDINAL: A person, usually a bishop, selected by the Pope to belong to a special group in the leadership of the Church.

CARDINAL VIRTUES: The four main virtues or habits of good actions. They are prudence, justice, temperance, and fortitude.

CATHOLIC: Universal.

CELIBACY: The state of life for those who have chosen to remain unmarried for the sake of the Kingdom of Heaven in order to give themselves entirely to God and to the service of his people.

CHOSEN PEOPLE: The Jewish people.

CHURCH MILITANT: The members of the Church on earth.

CHURCH SUFFERING: The souls in purgatory.

CHURCH TEACHING: The official teachings of the Catholic Church, which is given by the Pope and the bishops in union with him.

CHURCH TRIUMPHANT: The saints in heaven.

CIVIL LAW: Human laws made by those in civil authority.

CLERGY: The group of clerics, or ordained ministers (bishops, priests, or deacons).

COMMON GOOD: The welfare of the whole community and not just an individual.

COMMUNION OF SAINTS: The relationship that exists between all of the members of the Church, whether they are in heaven, in purgatory, or on earth. Those in heaven pray for us and help us in our needs. They also pray for those in purgatory. The souls in purgatory pray for us too. We can help them by our own prayers on their behalf. Belief in the Communion of Saints is quite ancient in the Church, going back to the times of the apostles. The word *saint* here means anyone who is in the state of sanctifying grace.

CONSCIENCE: The ability we have to judge right from wrong according to what we have learned from faith and reason. For a person to have a *good conscience*, he must study the Bible and the teachings of the Church and put them into practice.

CONTEMPLATIVE: Those who lead a cloisterd life, completely separated from the world, in order to pray for the world. They work within their monasteries or communities to support themselves.

COUNTER-REFORMATION: The period of Catholic reform during the sixteenth and early seventeenth centuries, in which new saints and new religious orders were formed to eliminate corruption in the Church and to oppose the rise of Protestantism. Also known as the Catholic Reformation.

CRUSADES: The military efforts of Western Christians, from the eleventh through the thirteenth centuries, to retake the Holy Land from Muslim control.

CURIA: The body of officials who assist a bishop (diocesan curia) or the Pope (the Roman curia) in governing a diocese or the universal Church.

DEPOSIT OF FAITH: The content of revelation entrusted to the Church by Jesus Christ and handed on through the Scripture and Tradition by the apostles and their successors.

DEPOSIT OF GRACE: All the grace necessary for salvation which Jesus merited for us by his death.

DEVELOPMENT OF DOCTRINE: Growth in the understanding of God's revelation, which continues through the contemplation and study of believers, theological research, and the preaching of the Magisterium.

DIOCESE: The part of the Church over which a bishop has authority.

DIVINE LAW: The moral law which comes to us from God.

DIVINE OFFICE: The prayer of the Church using psalms, hymns, and readings. It is called the Liturgy of the Hours because parts of it may be prayed at different times of the day.

DOCTORS OF THE CHURCH: Saints whose writings are acknowledged by the Church for their enduring theological and spiritual value.

ECCLESIASTICAL LAW: Laws made by Church authorities.

ECUMENISM: Cooperation among Christians, including efforts to restore full unity in truth and love among all Christians.

EKKLESIA: Greek word for assembly which is used in the New Testament for the Church.

ENCYCLICAL: A pastoral letter written by the Pope and sent to the whole Church to express Church teaching on some important matter.

ETERNAL LAW: The law by which God governs all things, directing and ordering each to its proper end or purpose.

EUCHARIST: The real Body and Blood of Jesus under the appearances of bread and wine.

EVANGELICAL COUNSELS: The teachings of the New Law proposed by Jesus to his disciples which lead to the perfection of Christian life. They are poverty, celibacy, and obedience.

EX CATHEDRA: A Latin expression that means "from the chair" and refers to the authority of the Pope when he teaches infallibly.

FATHERS OF THE CHURCH: Early Christian writers of the early centuries whose writings and teachings are the earliest expressions of the Tradition of the Church.

FIAT: A Latin word meaning "let it be done"; it is the Latin translation of Mary's words to the angel Gabriel when she was asked to be the Mother of God.

FILIAL PIETY: The virtue of children giving honor and respect to their parents and those in authority.

GENERAL JUDGMENT: The universal judgment of the entire human race at the end of the world.

GENTILE: A person of a non-Jewish nation or of non-Jewish faith.

GRACE: The free gift that God gives us by which he helps us to reach heaven. There are different kinds of graces: sanctifying, sacramental, and actual.

GREAT WESTERN SCHISM: The conflict that ran from 1378-1417 in which two men and later three men at the same time claimed to be Pope. Catholics were confused and divided over who was the true Pope. The Council of Constance ended the schism.

HABIT: A way of acting that is usually acquired by repetition of certain actions.

HERESIES: Religious beliefs that corrupt the true teachings of Christ and the Church. Those who teach or believe these false ideas are called *heretics*.

HIERARCHY: The order of authority in the Church. The bishops united under the Pope as the true successors of Saint Peter and the apostles form the *hierarchy* in the Church. It is their duty to teach the faith, govern Christians in their dioceses, and administer the sacraments.

HOLINESS: Being close to or belonging to God.

ICON: Means "image" and refers to religious images used in the devotion of Eastern Christians.

IMMACULATE CONCEPTION: Mary's conception free of the stain of original sin. Through the grace of God, Mary was free from original sin from the moment of her conception.

IMMORTAL: To be free from death. The soul of every human being is immortal, that is, it will never die. When death comes to the body, the soul lives on in heaven, purgatory, or hell.

IMPECCABILITY: Not capable of sinning or liable to sin.

INFALLIBILITY: The truth that the Catholic Church, by the special help of the Holy Spirit, is kept free from any error in teaching us about what we must believe (faith) and how we must live (morals). Only the Pope, or all the bishops united under the Pope, can teach us *infallibly*.

INTERCEDE: To speak in the interests of another person or to ask something for another person.

INTERCESSORY PRAYER: Prayer on behalf of another person.

JUST WAR: The legitimate and just military effort of a nation that must defend itself from an unjust aggressor after every other effective means has been used.

LAITY: All those baptized members of the Church who are not clergy or in a religious state of life.

LITURGICAL YEAR: The celebration throughout the year of the mysteries of the Lord's birth, life, death, and Resurrection in such a way that the entire year becomes a "year of the Lord's grace."

LITURGY: The public ceremonies of the Church used for worship.

MAGISTERIUM: The teaching office or authority in the Church. The magisterium is exercised by the Pope and the bishops united with him. By Christ's command, all Christians are solemnly obliged to obey the teachings of the magisterium.

MARTYR: A witness to the truth of the Faith, in which the person endures even death to be faithful to Christ.

MENTAL PRAYER: Prayer that is said interiorly which unites our hearts with God while we meditate on his holy truths.

MIDDLE AGES: The period of European history from the fall of Rome in the fifth century to the beginning of the Italian Renaissance in the fifteenth century.

MODERNISM: The teachings that faith and morals change and there is no concrete, objective right and wrong along with the desire for the supernatural.

MONASTERIES: The communities where monks live according to a specific rule or way of life.

MONSIGNOR: A title of honor given to certain members of the clergy.

MONSTRANCE: The sacred vessel in which the consecrated Host is placed for exposition or Benediction of the Blessed Sacrament.

MORAL LAW: God's eternal law which directs our will towards the good.

MYSTICAL BODY OF CHRIST: the Church; the union of the members of the Church with each other and Christ.

NATURAL LAW: The basic moral law which God has placed in human nature and which we discover through reason.

PARTICULAR JUDGMENT: The individual judgment by Christ of each human being at the moment after death.

PATRIOTISM: Rightly ordered love of one's country.

PATRON SAINTS: The saints after whom we are named at Baptism and at Confirmation. These saints pray for us in a special way and help us to reach heaven. We should learn about our patron saints and try to love God as they did.

PENTECOST: The special feast of the Holy Spirit. It recalls the coming of the Spirit upon the apostles. We celebrate Pentecost fifty days after Easter.

PERPETUAL VIRGINITY: The doctrine that Mary was always a virgin: before, during and after the birth of Christ.

PILGRIM CHURCH: Another title for the Church. It reminds us that we are *pilgrims*, that is, people who are on a spiritual journey to the Kingdom of God. It reminds us that life on earth is only a temporary thing, and that heaven is our true home.

POLYTHEISM: Belief in many gods.

POPE: The visible leader of the Church and supreme teacher of the Catholic faith. The Pope receives his authority from Christ as a successor of Saint Peter. All Catholics are obliged to respect and obey the Pope as the representative of Christ for the whole Church.

PRIMACY: Means "first place."

PROTESTANT REFORMATION: The sixteenth century movement whose leaders included Martin Luther and John Calvin, and that began by trying to reform genuine evils in the Catholic Church but which eventually rejected many of the Church's teachings and broke away from the Catholic Church.

RENAISSANCE: Means "rebirth" and refers to the rediscovery of classical antiquity in the period of the fourteenth century through the seventeenth century.

REVELATION: the truths of faith which God has made known to us through Scripture and tradition.

RITE (RITES): 1. A rite is a particular way of celebrating the sacraments according to the rules of the Church. For example, there is a detailed *rite* for baptizing people. 2. Rite can also mean a whole group of Christians who share a common way of worship and of living the faith. There are five different rites or kinds of Catholics in the Church. All of us profess the same faith. The two largest rites are the Roman Catholics and the Byzantine Catholics.

SACRAMENT: A visible sign or ceremony given to us by Jesus in order to give us sanctifying grace. There are seven sacraments in the Church: Baptism, Confirmation, Holy Eucharist, Penance, Anointing, Holy Orders, and Matrimony.

SACRAMENTS OF INITIATION: The sacraments of Baptism, Holy Eucharist, and Confirmation, by which Christians are fully incorporated into the Church.

SACRED SCRIPTURE: The Bible.

SECOND COMING: The return of Jesus at the end of the world as he promised at his Ascension.

SEPERATED BRETHREN: Fellow Christians who are separated from full unity with the Catholic Church. Included among the separated brethren are Orthodox Christians and Protestants of various kinds, including Baptists, Episcopalians, Lutherans, Methodists, and Presbyterians.

SENSUM FIDELIUM: Means "The sense of the faithful" and refers to what the faithful have believed over the centuries.

ST. ATHANASIUS: Bishop of Alexandria in the fourth century who defended the truth that Jesus is God.

ST. AUGUSTINE: He lived in the fourth century, and due to the persistent prayers of his mother, Monica, he converted to Catholicism. Before his conversion, he led a sinful life. After his conversion he became a great teacher, bishop, and theologian and wrote many works. He is a saint and Doctor of the Church.

ST. BENEDICT: He lived in the 5th century and is called the "Father of Western Monasticism". He founded the Benedictine Order. He also wrote the Rule of St. Benedict, which is a guide for the daily life of his monks.

ST. CATHERINE OF SIENA: A very holy Italian woman from the fourteenth century who convinced the Pope to return to Rome after having moved to Avignon, France. She also wrote much and is a Doctor of the Church.

ST. DOMINIC: A Spaniard from the twelfth century who founded the Order of Preachers, which is now commonly referred to as the Dominican Order. He was sent to convert the Albigensians (heretics of that time) and promoted devotion to the Rosary.

ST. FRANCIS OF ASSISI: A wealthy, reckless Italian youth from the thirteenth century who had a powerful conversion to Christianity. He gave up everything to live as a poor man and follow Jesus. He started the Franciscan Order.

ST. IGNATIUS OF LOYOLA: The founder of the Society of Jesus (or Jesuits) whose mission is to defend and serve the Pope and to educate people in the Catholic faith.

ST. THOMAS AQUINAS: An Italian Dominican from the thirteenth century who was a brilliant philosopher and theologian. He is a doctor of the Church and was given the title "The Angelic Doctor" for his brilliant writings and great love of God and neighbor.

STEWARDSHIP: Caring for creation and using wisely the gifts God has given us.

SYNOD: A meeting of bishops of an ecclesiastical province to discuss the doctrinal and pastoral needs of the Church.

THEOLOGIAN: Someone who studies God and religion.

TRADITION: The teachings of Christ that were preached by the apostles and handed down from century to century.

VENERATE: To show devotion, respect, and honor to Mary, the apostles, martyrs, saints, holy objects, places, etc.

VESTMENTS: One of the articles of the ceremonial attire and insignia worn by ecclesiastical officiants and assistants as indicative of their rank and appropriate to the rite being celebrated.

VICAR: A representative; one serving as an agent for someone else.

VIRTUE: A good habit that we learn which helps us to do good and avoid evil. Some virtues are prudence, justice, temperance, fortitude, humility, chastity, and prayer.

VOCAL PRAYER: Prayer that is expressed by spoken words with the participation of the mind and heart.

VOCATION: The calling or destiny we have in this life and hereafter.

Prayers

THE SIGN OF THE CROSS

In the name of the Father, and of the Son, and of the Holy Spirit. *Amen.*

OUR FATHER

Our Father who art in heaven, hallowed be thy name. Thy kingdom come. Thy will be done on earth, as it is in heaven. Give us this day our daily bread, and forgive us our trespasses, as we forgive those who trespass against us, and lead us not into temptation, but deliver us from evil. *Amen.*

HAIL MARY

Hail Mary, full of grace, the Lord is with thee. Blessed art thou among women, and blessed is the fruit of thy womb, Jesus.

Holy Mary, Mother of God, pray for us sinners now and at the hour of our death. *Amen.*

GLORY BE

Glory be to the Father, and to the Son, and to the Holy Spirit. As it was in the beginning, is now, and ever shall be, world without end. *Amen.*

MORNING OFFERING

O Jesus, through the Immaculate Heart of Mary I offer thee my prayers, works, joys, and sufferings of this day in union with the Holy Sacrifice of the Mass throughout the world.

I offer them for all the intentions of thy Sacred Heart: the salvation of souls, reparation for sin, the reunion of all Christians.

I offer them for the intentions of our Bishops and of all Apostles of Prayer, and in particular for those recommended by our Holy Father this month. *Amen.*

THE APOSTLES' CREED

I believe in God,
    the Father Almighty,
    creator of heaven and earth.
I believe in Jesus Christ,
    his only Son, our Lord.
He was conceived by the power of the
    Holy Spirit
    and born of the Virgin Mary.
He suffered under Pontius Pilate,
    was crucified, died, and was buried.
    He descended into hell.
On the third day he rose again.
He ascended into heaven
    and is seated at the right
    hand of the Father.
    He will come again to judge
    the living and the dead.
I believe in the Holy Spirit,
    the holy catholic Church,
    the communion of saints,
    the forgiveness of sins,
    the resurrection of the body,
    and the life everlasting. *Amen.*

ACT OF FAITH

O my God, I firmly believe that thou art one God in three Divine Persons: Father, Son, and Holy Spirit. I believe that thy Divine Son became man and died for our sins, and that he will come to judge the living and the dead. I believe these and all the truths that the Holy Catholic Church teaches, because thou hast revealed them, who can neither deceive nor be deceived. *Amen.*

ACT OF HOPE

O my God, relying on thy infinite goodness and promises, I hope to obtain pardon of my sins, the help of thy grace, and life everlasting, through the merits of Jesus Christ, my Lord and Redeemer. *Amen.*

ACT OF LOVE

O my God, I love thee above all things, with my whole heart and soul, because thou art all good and worthy of all my love. I love my neighbor as myself for the love of thee. I forgive all who have injured me and ask pardon of all whom I have injured. *Amen.*

ACT OF CONTRITION

O my God, I am heartily sorry for having offended thee. I detest all my sins because of thy just punishments, but most of all because they offend thee, my God, who art all good and deserving of all my love. I firmly resolve, with the help of thy grace, to confess my sins, to do penance, and to amend my life. *Amen.*

THE ANGELUS

V. The angel of the Lord declared unto Mary.
R. And she conceived of the Holy Spirit.

Hail Mary. . . .

V. Behold the handmaid of the Lord.
R. Be it done to me according to thy word.

Hail Mary. . . .

V. And the Word was made flesh.
R. And dwelt among us.

Hail Mary. . . .
V. Pray for us, O holy Mother of God.

R. That we may be made worthy of the promises of Christ.

Let us pray. Pour forth, we beseech thee, O Lord, thy grace into our hearts, that we, to whom the Incarnation of Christ thy Son was made known by the message of an angel, may by his Passion and Cross be brought to the glory of his Resurrection. Through the same Christ our Lord. *Amen.*

MYSTERIES OF THE ROSARY

The Joyful Mysteries

1. The Annunciation.
2. The Visitation.
3. The Nativity.
4. The Presentation.
5. The Finding in the Temple.

The Sorrowful Mysteries

1. The Agony in the Garden.
2. The Scourging at the Pillar.
3. The Crowning with Thorns.
4. The Carrying of the Cross.
5. The Crucifixion.

The Glorious Mysteries

1. The Resurrection.
2. The Ascension.
3. The Descent of the Holy Spirit.
4. The Assumption.
5. The Coronation.

Optional: The Luminous Mysteries

1. The Baptism of Christ in the Jordan.
2. The Wedding Feast of Cana.
3. The Proclamation of the Kingdom of God.
4. The Transfiguration of Our Lord.
5. The Institution of the Holy Eucharist.

LITANY OF LORETO

Lord, have mercy on us.
Christ, have mercy on us.
Lord, have mercy on us.
Christ, hear us.
Christ, graciously hear us.
God the Father of heaven,
have mercy on us.
God the Son, Redeemer of the world,
have mercy on us.
God the Holy Spirit,
have mercy on us.
Holy Trinity, One God,
have mercy on us.

Holy Mary, *pray for us.**
Holy Mother of God,
Holy Virgin of virgins,
Mother of Christ,
Mother of divine grace,
Mother most pure,
Mother most chaste,
Mother inviolate,
Mother undefiled,
Mother most amiable,
Mother most admirable,
Mother of good counsel,
Mother of the Church,
Mother of our Creator,
Mother of our Savior,
Virgin most prudent,
Virgin most venerable,
Virgin most renowned,
Virgin most powerful,
Virgin most merciful,
Virgin most faithful,
Mirror of justice,
Seat of wisdom,
Cause of our joy,
Spiritual vessel,

Pray for us is repeated after each invocation.

Vessel of honor,
Singular vessel of devotion,
Mystical rose,
Tower of David,
Tower of ivory,
House of gold,
Ark of the covenant,
Gate of heaven,
Morning star,
Health of the sick,
Refuge of sinners,
Comforter of the afflicted,
Help of Christians,
Queen of Angels,
Queen of Patriarchs,
Queen of Prophets,
Queen of Apostles,
Queen of Martyrs,
Queen of Confessors,
Queen of Virgins,
Queen of all Saints,
Queen conceived without original sin,
Queen assumed into heaven,
Queen of the most holy Rosary,
Queen of peace,

Lamb of God, who take away the sins of the world, *spare us, O Lord.*
Lamb of God, who take away the sins of the world, *graciously hear us, O Lord.*
Lamb of God, who take away the sins of the world, *have mercy on us.*

Pray for us, O holy Mother of God.
That we may be made worthy of the promises of Christ.

Let us pray: Grant, we beseech Thee, O Lord God, unto us Thy servants, that we may rejoice in continual health of mind and body; and, by the glorious intercession of blessed Mary ever Virgin, may be delivered from present sadness, and enter into the joy of Thine eternal gladness. Through Christ our Lord. *Amen.*

THE STATIONS OF THE CROSS

1. Jesus is condemned to death.
2. Jesus carries his Cross.
3. Jesus falls the first time.
4. Jesus meets his mother.
5. Jesus is helped by Simon of Cyrene.
6. Veronica wipes the face of Jesus.
7. Jesus falls a second time.
8. Jesus speaks to the women.
9. Jesus falls a third time.
10. Jesus is stripped of his clothes.
11. Jesus is nailed to the Cross.
12. Jesus dies on the Cross.
13. Jesus is taken down from the Cross.
14. Jesus is placed in the tomb.

PRAYER FOR THE POPE

Father of Providence, look with love on *N.* our Pope, your appointed successor to St. Peter on whom you built your Church. May he be the visible center and foundation of our unity in faith and love. Grant this through Our Lord Jesus Christ, your Son, who lives and reigns with you and the Holy Spirit, one God, for ever and ever. *Amen.*

PRAYER FOR A BISHOP

Lord our God, you have chosen your servant *N.* to be a shepherd of your flock in the tradition of the apostles. Give him a spirit of courage and right judgment, a spirit of knowledge and love. By governing with fidelity those entrusted to his care may he build your Church as a sign of salvation for the world. We ask this through Our Lord Jesus Christ, your Son, who lives and reigns with you and the Holy Spirit, one God, for ever and ever. *Amen.*

PRAYER FOR VOCATIONS
by POPE JOHN PAUL II

O Jesus, our Good Shepherd, bless all our parishes with numerous priests, deacons, men and women in religious life, consecrated laity and missionaries, according to the needs of the entire world, which you love and wish to save.

We especially entrust our community to you; grant us the spirit of the first Christians, so that we may be a cenacle of prayer, in loving acceptance of the Holy Spirit and his gifts.

Assist our pastors and all who live a consecrated life. Guide the steps of those who have responded generously to your call and are preparing to receive holy orders or to profess the evangelical counsels.

Look with love on so many well-disposed young people and call them to follow you. Help them to understand that in you alone can they attain to complete fulfillment.

To this end we call on the powerful intercession of Mary, Mother and Model of all vocations. We beseech you to sustain our faith with the certainty that the Father will grant what you have commanded us to ask. *Amen.*

PRAYER FOR
UNITY OF THE CHURCH

Almighty and merciful God, you willed that the different nations should become one people through your Son. Grant in your kindness that those who glory in being known as Christians may put aside their differences and become one in truth and charity, and that all men, enlightened by the true faith, may be united in fraternal communion in the one Church. Through Christ Our Lord. *Amen.*

ANIMA CHRISTI

Soul of Christ, sanctify me.
Body of Christ, save me.
Blood of Christ, inebriate me.
Water from the side of Christ, wash me.
Passion of Christ, strengthen me.
O good Jesus, hear me;
Within thy wounds hide me;
Suffer me not to be separated from thee;
From the malignant enemy defend me;
In the hour of my death call me,
And bid me come to Thee,
That with Thy Saints I may praise Thee
for ever and ever. *Amen.*

MEMORARE

Remember, O most gracious Virgin Mary, that never was it known that anyone who fled to thy protection, implored thy help, or sought thy intercession, was left unaided. Inspired with this confidence, I fly unto thee, O Virgin of Virgins, my Mother: to thee do I come, before thee I stand, sinful and sorrowful. O Mother of the Word Incarnate, despise not my petitions, but in thy mercy hear and answer me. *Amen.*

PRAYER TO ST. MICHAEL

St. Michael, the Archangel, defend us in battle. Be our protection against the wickedness and snares of the devil. May God rebuke him, we humbly pray, and do thou, O prince of the heavenly hosts, by the power of God, thrust into hell Satan and the other evil spirits who prowl about the world seeking the ruin of souls. *Amen.*

EXAMINATION OF CONSCIENCE

How have I acted toward God? Do I think of God and speak to Him by praying to Him each day?

Do I speak of God with reverence?

Do I go to Mass on Sunday?

Do I do all I can to make Sunday a day of rest and joy for my family?

Do I participate in Mass, or do I tease or distract others by laughing, talking, or playing?

Do I pay attention to my parents, priests, and teachers when they talk to me about God?

How have I acted toward others?

Do I obey my parents and teachers quickly and cheerfully, or must I be reminded many times?

Do I tell my parents or those in authority over me that I am sorry and ask them to forgive me when I have not minded them?

Do I obey the rules of my home and school?

Do I help my brothers, sisters, and classmates when they need my help?

Am I kind to everyone?

Did I hit, kick, or in any way hurt others on purpose?

Am I willing to play with everyone?

Did I make fun or say mean things to anyone?

Do I do all my classwork and my chores at home well?

Do I take care of my health by eating the right food, etc.?

Do I think or do bad things or say bad words?

Do I tell the truth?

Do I say things about other people that are not true?

Did I cheat in class or in a game?

Did I steal or keep things that are not mine?

Am I willing to share my things with others?

Do I return things that I have borrowed?

THE PRAYER OF FATIMA

O my Jesus, forgive us our sins, save us from the fires of hell, and lead all souls into heaven, especially those in most need of thy mercy. *Amen.*

SPIRITUAL COMMUNION

My Jesus, as I cannot receive thee now in the Most Holy Blessed Sacrament, I ask thee to come into my heart, and make it like thy heart. *Amen.*

PRAYER TO MY GUARDIAN ANGEL

Angel of God, my guardian dear, To whom God's love commits me here, Ever this day be at my side, To light and guard, to rule and guide. *Amen.*

Abbreviations

AA   *Apostolicam actuositatem* (Decree on the Apostolate of the Laity), November 18, 1965.

CCC   *Catechism of the Catholic Church*, 2nd ed., 1997.

DH   *Dignitatis humanae* (Declaration on Religious Liberty), December 7, 1965.

DV   *Dei verbum* (Dogmatic Constitution on Divine Revelation), November 18, 1965.

FC   *Familiaris consortio* (The Role of the Christian Family in the Modern World), November 22, 1981.

GS   *Gaudium et spes* (Pastoral Constitution on the Church in the Modern World), December 7, 1965.

LG   *Lumen gentium* (Dogmatic Constitution on the Church), November 21, 1964.

MD   *Mediator Dei*, November 20, 1947 (Encyclical of Pius XII).

OE   *Orientalium Ecclesiarum* (Decree on the Catholic Eastern Churches), November 21, 1964.

PC   *Perfectae caritatis* (Decree on the Up-to-date Renewal of Religious Life), October 28, 1965.

SC   *Sacrosanctum concilium* (Constitution on the Sacred Liturgy), December 4, 1963.

UR   *Unitatis redintegratio* (Decree on Ecumenism), November 21, 1964.

Art Credits

ILLUSTRATIONS, CHRISTOPHER J. PELICANO:
pages 38, 53, 87, 109, 119, 120, 128, 133, 150, 167, 171

PHOTOGRAPHS

Oblates of the Blessed Virgin Mary, Boston: 40, 117
Victor Puccetti: 33, 91, 140
Gary Fuchs: 44, 152
Sisters of the Immaculate Heart, Wichita: 116
Spiering: 105
Martha Brown: 127
Stock, Boston:
Herb Snitzer: 90
Bill Gallery: 102
Owen Franken: 121
Milton Feinberg: 122
J. Howard: 130